A DARK STRANGER'S GUIDE TO THE ISLE OF MAN

By Kerron Cross

A short humorous book on the Isle of Man based on over 30 years of visiting the island. Aimed at the (massive) Manx tourist market, the book talks about everything that is good about Ellan Vannin in a style similar to Bill Bryson, but much better. And much less ginger.

Chapters:

Introduction – A short introduction as to why I want to write a travel writing style book on the Isle of Man. It's certainly never been done before! (Page 4)

Chapter 1 – Trains, Boats and Planes. Answering the question: *"How do you get to the Isle of Man?"* (Page 9)

Chapter 2 – Douglas. Highlighting all that is great about the island's capital. (Page 21)

Chapter 3 – Laxey. My favourite seaside resort in the world, in spite of the lack of sand. Also a focus on the mining traditions and the allure of The Lady Isabella. (Page 41)

Chapter 4 – Ramsey. Queenie fishing and the Mooragh Park. (Page 61)

Introduction –

So why write a book about the Isle of Man?

I guess at a very basic level, the Island has always been in my DNA. My Mum was Manx – actually she still is, last time I checked – and we still visit friends and relatives fairly regularly.

For the first 30 years of my life, it was where we spent our two week Summer Holiday. Not for us the sunshine of Greece or Spain – no, we enjoyed walking the glens and freezing on the front at Laxey. Genuinely, we did. Perhaps we needed to get out more. That is where the attraction began.

A quick glance at the front of the book will tell you that I have a Manx name. Yes, it is meant to be spelt like that – and, yes, it is a boy's name. *"Kerron"* means *"Dark Stranger"*. At least this is what I was told from a young age – with the invention of the internet it is easier now to whizz around from A to Z and find that this is not what most Manx or Celtic name books say my name means. However, in a race between who I believe more, my mother or Wikipedia, I will side with my Mum every time.

Someone told me (and no, it wasn't my Mum, before you ask), that my name probably dates back to before the Viking invasions. When seeing strangers with dark hair (Celts) was perceived to be a good thing and that seeing strangers with blonde hair (Vikings) was perceived to be a bad thing. I don't mean that to sound like a racial slur – some of my best friends are Scandinavians – I fully expect that these invaders could be delightful company of an evening down the local hostelry once you got to know them, but it might just be that you had to survive an axe in the back of the head if you met them out on Peel beach of a dark night.

Although logic dictates if you were Manx, a dark night would probably be much better than a bright one.

The name even inspired me to back a horse in the 2000 Grand National. I couldn't believe my luck when I saw the words *"Dark Stranger"* staring back at me out of the newspaper. It must be fate. A 9-1 favourite ridden by Champion Jockey A.P. McCoy, what could possibly go wrong...well, in hindsight, quite a lot. Poor old *"Dark Stranger"* fell at the third fence. I felt cheated, but I am sure the bookies felt elated.

And that's not the only tenuous link to near-greatness in this book though. Oh no.

My family were related by marriage to Ned Maddrell.

At this point I should explain a couple of things: 1) Being related by marriage is a bit like saying *"not related at all"*. 2) Ned Maddrell was the last ever native Manx speaker, and not the old lady who used to be in Neighbours.

From a young age I would learn to describe myself as *"British"* rather than *"English"* – a small act of solidarity that no doubt filled my family and friends with great pride/bemusement in equal measure.

Having gone on to grow up and marry a Glaswegian though, it is these kinds of small distinction that keep you alive. *"He's not English, he's Manx"* and *"Don't worry, you'll be fine...so long as you don't speak"* are the sort of the phrases I hear bandied about when I'm North of the Border. There are no such concerns on the Isle of Man – it is a small but independent kingdom safely marooned between its neighbours Scotland, England, Wales, Northern Ireland and the Republic of Ireland, providing an eclectic mix of accents, languages and cultural identities which make it the great place it is today.

There is a real sense of belonging too. I can still be approached by random people on the island (this is mainly OK, so long as they have dark hair) saying *"You're Bob Wright's Grandson!"* Whilst this is undeniably true, I should probably add that I have not seen my Grandad since I was 4 years old – based mainly on the fact that he rather annoyingly and inconsiderately died.

I would have a much better book if he was still alive today. Indeed, given that he would be nearly 120 years old it would be a fantastic read for anyone to pick up. But let us put such things to one side for now. It is fair to say that my memories of him are blurry at best – and not just because of the perpetual fug of pipe smoke which used to surround him.

It's nice that people still remember him. Perhaps it is because the island is a small place where most people know each other. Perhaps it's because not much has happened to talk of since 1981. Or perhaps it's because he was a Mason, I don't know, but I can say I never learnt the handshake.

So this is where our adventure begins. A return to the old country and an explanation why I have a continuing love affair with Ellan Vannin.

1. Trains, Boats and Planes

First question you have to answer when holidaying in the Isle of Man is: *"How do you get to the Isle of Man?"* It's an important question, and one which shouldn't be overlooked.

Half the adventure of a holiday is the travelling – and if you are relying on British Rail to get there, it really is an adventure!

My dad spent his whole life working on the railways. We rarely had much money growing up – this was mainly due to the fact that my dad spent his whole life working on the railways.

One of the perks of a career at times being both metaphorically and literally in a siding with British Rail, is that you would get the promise of free travel.

Before the wondrous idea of privatisation, where 'competition' guaranteed that not only would your ticket price be expensive, but you wouldn't even know who to complain to if and when something went wrong – reassuring when you are sat at Stafford station at 3am –

all travel used to be provided centrally by good old British Rail. And when I say 'travel', I mean 'excuses'.

Our journey would usually begin at Watford Junction station. I'm not sure if you've been to Watford Junction station, but you've probably been through it. On reflection, it is undoubtedly best seen this way.

The boat taking us to the Isle of Man, annoyingly left from the North West of England – and not from the North West of London, just outside the M25. More's the pity. Actually the M25 wasn't even invented back then, so you'd have had to find somewhere else to park your car of a morning.

The trip up the West Coast Main Line (yes, you will get all the technical terms here) was a familiar one. Like an old friend. Well, like an old acquaintance you'd meet a couple of times a year when you didn't have any other choice.

For us, the route was familiar for two main reasons:

1) Travelling to the Isle of Man, for our two week holiday in the Summer.

2) Travelling to visit family in Wigan (*"Wigan North-Western, change here for Wigan Wallgate"*, not sure if anyone ever did).

Dad had developed an interesting patter for such journeys. Unsurprisingly, perhaps, this combined his geographical knowledge of all the key tourist sites of interest which were based on the West Coast Main Line – and all the major railway transport disasters of the last 100 years.

For example, we would hear great tales about The Fairy Castle, The Giant's Graveyard, the plastic cows at Milton Keynes, The Great Train Robbery and several train crashes where the driver and numerous passengers died. Happy days.

As seasoned travellers then, we would have a choice of two destinations from which to catch our connecting ferry to the Isle of Man. For the first few years I can remember, we would catch the boat from Liverpool (*"Change at Liverpool Lime Street for the Isle of Man ferry").*

Home of The Beatles, football (if you don't count Andy Gray's cheating header out of Steve Sherwood's hands for Everton versus Watford in the 1984 FA Cup Final – which, in fairness, most people don't) and shell-suits. In other words, culture personified.

The sea journey afforded unique views of the Liver Building, Blackpool Tower and a sunken banana boat that had run aground many years before.

It used to be that you could just turn up on the day and pick which of the two ferries to the Isle of Man to take that day. That's not the case now, you have to buy your tickets days/weeks in advance and hope the one sailing that day isn't booked up.

We always looked forward to travelling on the old style ferries run by the Isle of Man Steampacket Company. Those ships have a special place in my heart. Ben My Chree, Mona's Isle, Mona's Queen, Lady of Mann, Tynwald, Manx Maid and latterly the Manx

Viking (dual funnel, purchased from then rival Sealink).

Our first job would be to find a 'berth' down below deck for my Mum in the 'lounge' area. Old green leather couch style seats surrounded by old oak – so much more refined when you were being sick over them.

Apparently in the restaurant all the cutlery (best silver) and the condiments were embossed with 'Isle of Man Steampacket Company' on. (This is what companies did in the olden days, as a sign of quality – nowadays you only see such moves by companies trying to prevent low level theft.) I say 'apparently' because we could never afford to eat in the restaurant – our fine dining experience was based around homemade sandwiches and hard boiled eggs (peel on the day for extra flavour).

Out on deck I would go with my dad as the boat left harbour. As the ship's horn wailed my dad would hold me close and jovially say: *"That's the ship saying 'Bye-bye, Liverpool'".* In fact what my Dad was really saying was: *"I have no real explanation for this loud noise, but please do not cry/soil yourself/tell your mother"*.

But the Liverpool experience of my childhood only lasted so long. By my teens we were instead making the journey from Heysham Port. I'm not sure if you've ever been to Heysham, but it's fair to say that it isn't going to win European Capital of Culture anytime soon.

The only thing that appeared to be at Heysham, apart from the port (and obligatory railway station) was a giant nuclear reactor. I think if I had to pick a word, it would be 'foreboding'. The giant sign on the side of the port building said 'TERMINAL' in six foot high letters. It was hard to argue with this witheringly astute observation about the health of the site – it wasn't clear what it had been ill with, but Heysham wasn't recovering anytime soon. It certainly wasn't going to be fixed with a lick of paint and some embossed cutlery.

I imagine that our change from Liverpool to Heysham wasn't aesthetically driven, though the bright neon 'electric eels' at Heysham were unarguably colourful. Far more likely that it was due to the fact that it was cheaper, although around the same time the Steampacket Company in their wisdom had cut back on the number of old style ferries it owned, and instead had ventured out into buying a Seacat.

I am presuming that most of you know what a Seacat is, but for those of you who aren't familiar with them, I should point out this is not a fluffy animal with whiskers, but rather a new-fangled hydrofoil/catamaran style of boat. Quicker and more compact than a ferry, it brings the joy of airline style travel to the waves. Imagine not being allowed on deck, whilst being crammed into tight rows of seating with minimal legroom for hours on end, with the faint aroma of wee and vomit greeting you at every turn.

The travel experience is not helped by the feeling that every time someone farts the boat is going to go up and down on the sea like a jet-ski doing aerial tricks at Waikiki. Given that the Irish Sea is not the calmest of seas at the best of times, this would lead to some horror crossings or occasions when the sailing was cancelled altogether. When this is your one holiday of the year, such risks can't be taken lightly.

Liverpool generally had the Seacat, Heysham would generally have some kind of ferry – maybe not an old style one, but even the freight sailing on a big boat filled with equally big truckers was considered preferable to the alternative.

For the middle of the journey we would retreat indoors – not to the now eradicated leather and oak lounge area or restaurant, but to the café/bar/shop area – the only area with seats with any real legroom and tables on which to play cards, or position children's puzzle books. This was our opportunity to warm up and to see Mum, as around an hour away from our arrival in Douglas (capital of the Isle of Man and not the name of one of the truckers) we would go back out on deck to try and get our first glimpse of the year of our island hideaway – and take some relief from the fact that this part of the journey was nearly over.

As we pulled into Douglas Bay the ship's horn would sound once more: *"Hello,*

Douglas!" was the translation my dad attributed to this sound.

At the mouth of the harbour stands 'The Tower of Refuge', a small castle built on Conister Rock – an outcrop of naturally forming, but extremely dangerous, rocks lying in the sea directly in front of the harbour entrance. These rocks had claimed their fair share of casualties before the castle was erected in 1832, by Sir William Hillary, following the loss of the Steampacket St George in 1830 in which he had commanded the lifeboat before he was washed overboard.

It is claimed that even to this day the castle is stocked daily with bread and fresh water for any shipwrecked persons – though they probably don't bother with a spare set of dry clothes for Sir William anymore.

Nobody actually died in the sinking of the St George, but I am assured that the disaster wasn't caused by the captain of the Isle of Man ferry leaning on the horn without his dad being able to explain what this scary noise was that had come out without warning or translation.

This port used to be the hub of the thriving Manx tourist industry. You can see old photos where the two main piers here were full of as many as nine Steampacket ferries at a time. Now you would do well to see two at once.

There used to be daily arrivals from places like Stranraer, Belfast, Holyhead, Dublin, Fleetwood (nicknamed the 'Fleetwood Funboat') and, of course, Heysham and Liverpool. Demand has undoubtedly peaked.

Gone is the message which was painted on the harbour wall to greet visitors: *"Failte Ellan Vannin"*. Which loosely translated from the original Manx Gaelic means: *"Hello tourists – please spend some money on our commemorative fudge"*.

Of course, taking a ferry is not the only way to get to the Isle of Man. You could always travel by plane. For us, such an option was a distant luxury which could only be dreamt of.

In my childhood, a trip on Manx Airlines was something that was as likely to occur as playing polo on a unicorn. Despite growing up in the Home Counties, I can tell you that such an occurrence was still not that likely.

You would fly in from such exotic locations as Liverpool, Manchester, Leeds-Bradford or, in our case, Luton. It was only when I was well into adulthood that I could afford to take such a flight. To say my expectations were on the high side is something of an understatement.

Affectionately known as *"the tin box"* ride, there were no drinks or sandwiches served. Although it was much swifter than a four hour ferry ride, there was equally as much chance of bringing your packed lunch up over yourself. The short ride often had its ups and downs – I think the technical term for this is 'turbulence'.

Manx Airlines was dead in the water (no pun intended) by the time I had the pleasure of flying, but still the plane would generally arrive in one piece at one of the many state of the art airports on the island.

OK, there is only one airport on the island and it isn't exactly large.

Ronaldsway Airport is what the industry may describe as 'boutique' in size. I can remember telling one of my childhood friends,

Aftab, that Ronaldsway was a massive airport with many terminals and a fantastic shopping experience. I based this mainly on the fact that at that point I had never actually been to Ronaldsway Airport.

I don't think Aftab ever made the short trip to the island, but I imagine if he had he would have been quite disappointed with the airport. For that I can only offer my sincere apologies. My enthusiasm was well meant.

Ronaldsway is a short taxi ride from Castletown. Which in itself is a short taxi ride from Douglas. Which in turn is a short taxi ride from pretty much everywhere else on the island. But don't let that put you off. You don't need a taxi to see the delights of this beautiful island.

Especially if you are staying in Douglas…

2. Douglas

There are plenty of places to stay in Douglas for the casual holidaymaker. If you took a quick glance down the Promenade, even from the misty deck of the Isle of Man ferry, you would see that the majority of buildings look like guesthouse accommodation.

During the Manx tourist boom of the 1950s and 1960s, the island was so popular with visitors from the UK and Ireland that special pleas had to be issued by the Government for people to turn their spare rooms into guest accommodation. As David Cameron might say, not so much a bedroom tax, more a spare room subsidy. But of course I am referring to the Manx Government here, rather than their counterparts at Westminster.

The edict was embraced with vigour by families up and down the island. Partly because the Manx people are generous and wonderfully hospitable, and partly because it meant much needed extra cash in the bank.

If you take a stroll into Douglas, away from the seafront and into the residential heart of the city, you can see that many of the terraced houses and semi-detached homes still have names above the door as if they were a holiday B&B. Most of these are not holiday B&Bs. I only say this in case you get the urge to knock on one of these doors after 11pm at night looking for a bed - chances are the reception you get will not be warm and welcoming.

The days of tourists flocking to the Isle of Man in large numbers ended many years ago. Cheap flights and holiday packages enabling ordinary working families to escape to sunnier climes such as Spain and Greece put paid to the charming, yet freezing, allure of the Manx pearl glistening in the Irish Sea. It's a shame, but simple economics.

The island had to adapt, and it was a basic grasp on simple economics which encouraged the change of tack. A decision was taken to move away from a focus on the tourism industry and instead focus on things such as the banking and gambling industries (please note, for clarity, I am referring to banking and gambling as two entirely separate industries here - although recent economic history on the mainland may indicate otherwise). Nowadays the Isle of Man has something of a reputation for being a tax haven for rich exiles to harbour their hard won money without having to lose a large amount to the UK tax man.

Some might say - not me obviously because I don't want to lose half my readership in the first few pages - but people who have made their riches from society probably have a moral duty to pay their fair share back into it. Revolutionaries who shall not get further column inches in this book, I can tell you.

For the Isle of Man is not part of the UK. It has its own Parliament, its own laws, and its own tax raising powers. In fact it is one of the oldest democracies in the Western world.

Many of the towering 1950s grand guesthouses on Douglas Promenade are now offices or *'executive apartments'* - and the Lido has been replaced by a bowling alley. Modernisation has been slow and subtle, but the evidence is there if you look for it.

Part of the charm of Douglas is its Victorian appeal. It is as if it has been frozen in the 1950s and a lot of people like that. Yes, I know Victoria wasn't on the throne in 1950, but you get my general point.

At one end of the bay, beyond the Prom and high above the harbour, is Douglas Head. Nowadays it is home to the fabulous Manx Radio (hello guys, love your shows, please buy the book and promote it with your listeners!), but it is a quaint little spot that was very popular in the early 1900s.

There is a statue of Sir William Hillary, of Tower of Refuge fame, staring out over the bay. Sir William went on to establish the RNLI, you know. Yes, thank him for the lifeboats that are now so commonplace in British waters.

Next to this is something called a *'Camera Obscura'*. I have only ever seen two of these in all my time on this earth. One here in Douglas and the other on Midsomer Murders. I prefer this one because it overlooks the sea rather than an old English country village, and also because to my knowledge no-one has been brutally murdered here.

The Camera Obscura is, again, Victorian. Before the days of video cameras, iPads and mobile phones, people used to pass their time by walking along the Promenade (thus the word *'promenade'* being synonymous with a gentle stroll) and by going into the Camera Obscura to look at a series of ingenious mirrors and lenses which allowed them to see every aspect of the beautiful sea view. OK, I know it's got nothing on watching PJ and Duncan wrecking the mic on YouTube or Psy singing and dancing to Gangnam Style, but times were different back then. Joys, and technology, were simpler.

Of course, not all change is for the worse. Back in those days there used to be a world famous Black and White Minstrel Show. I won't go into the ins and outs of such performances, but fair to say it involved a large number of white men 'blacked up', to use the vernacular, for the entertainment of the middle classes. It's the sort of thing that the anti-discrimination brigade would have a field day with today - and rightly so.

A short walk down Marine Drive (over Douglas head and around the corner following the coast road) you would find Port Soderick. We went once, it was closed. Drenched from head to toe when we arrived, we huddled and shivered in a ramshackle shelter and waited an hour for the train to take us back to Douglas. Had it not been raining, what we would have seen is a beautiful bay, a Victorian walkway that has fallen into the sea and a restaurant owned by TV chef Kevin Woodford, which wasn't open. To be honest, I wouldn't bother with the walk down Marine Drive, but hey, it's up to you.

So back to Douglas. Halfway down the Prom is the Villa Marina. The Villa Marina is not, as it probably sounds, a place where the yachting classes tether their boats before they head down to the Casino. No, it's partly beautiful public gardens where you can take a pleasant stroll and eat ice cream whilst listening to the band at the bandstand (don't sit in the deck chairs, they will charge you) - and partly an old theatre style hall.

A few doors down is the more refined Gaiety Theatre, this is where you would go to see professional theatre productions such as Gilbert and Sullivan or an Evening With Ann Widdecombe (actually, not sure why you'd want to spend an evening with Ann Widdicombe, but whatever floats your boat, I suppose). I won't tell you the era of this theatre, but I'll give you a clue, it begins with a 'V'.

The Villa Marina is somewhere you would go during the height of Summer season. Maybe you would see Val Doonican or Les Dennis doing a turn. Ken Dodd came once and it sold out. But more generally the stage would be taken by things such as All Star British Wrestling with Big Daddy and Co, and other great delights you would more readily expect from a pier on the North West of England. These clever people knew their audience well.

However nearly every Summer of my childhood, the headline act at the Villa Marina would be The Great Ronricco. The windows, doors and surrounding telegraph poles would be plastered with posters advertising this great hypnotist/magician. He was no Derren Brown or Paul McKenna, but clearly had honed his act after many years working the audiences in Douglas. His face, staring out from the posters, was hypnotic. I guess that was the plan for a hypnotist. He looked like the guys off World Of The Strange, if you remember Trev and Simon's creation from Saturday morning's Going Live on BBC1. If you don't remember that, then think of Rolf Harris crossed with Colonel Sanders.

Ronricco - guessing that wasn't the name his mother gave him - was one of my earliest memories. Though because you had to be 18 to see his shows, it was many years before I would see him perform in person. I can remember being very impressed, particularly that he could win at noughts and crosses whilst blindfolded - I can't even do that without a blindfold. Canny man.

Around a hundred yards or so from the Villa Marina is a place where I would spend much of my holidays in the intervening years between being born and being allowed to witness Ronricco in action. We called it *'The Jumbo Shop'*.

The Jumbo Shop was actually called *'The Crescent Leisure Centre'* and was a giant amusement arcade - but at the back of it was a giant elephant, probably meant to be Dumbo, which me and my sister spent many years riding. I say *'riding'*, but given our precarious financial situation, I suspect we didn't put any money into the Jumbo machine we were simply allowed to sit on it while it was static. As I say, simple fun.

Many a happy hour was spent inside. When I was older I would play snooker and pool whilst watching MTV on the many TVs around the arcade. I would play Tekhan football with a giant rollerball that took all the skin off your hand, Derby Day with the two horses which were broken, and the penny falls games until they pushed them up to 10p a go.

I once saw Steve Guppy and Jon McCarthy from Port Vale FC playing pool. It was the place all the big name celebs would pop into to relax.

Next door was a waxworks museum. I was

always intrigued by the ghoulish looking Dracula figure, blood pouring from his mouth from where he had bitten the neck of a scantily clad blonde woman. I wasn't allowed in. Not sure of the age limit, but unlike Ronricco, by the time I was old enough to see what all the fuss was about it was no longer a waxwork museum and had instead been turned into a gym for weightlifters. Not quite the same attraction for a teenage boy - well, at least for this teenage boy, anyway.

The Crescent Leisure Centre was next door to the very swanky Empress Hotel. Another place I have never been to. Not sure I could afford to stay even today, but back in those days we would stay with Mum's family. It was lovely to see them and was also much much cheaper.

Grandad, Auntie Eva and Auntie Preston all lived in a house on Alexander Drive called *'Cronk Gennal'*. An idyllic little detached house with sweeping lawn at the front and extended gardens at the back where past the lawns were several plots for growing things like gooseberries, roses and green beans.

I wouldn't say they were self-sufficient, but it is worth reflecting that it is only recently that shops such as Tesco, McDonalds and KFC have made it into Douglas. Before that the nearest you had to these purveyors of gourmet luxury food was Shop Rite and Griddles burgers. Having said that, Marks and Spencers has long been a feature on Strand Street - how could any community in the developed world live without an olive and humous selection or a fine range of cardigans?

'Cronk Gennal' is Manx and it means 'Happy Hill' (Cronk is hill, Gennal is happy). It certainly was a happy place for us for two weeks of the year, and it was also on a hill. Good naming.

Whilst not that near the seafront, you could see why Grandad had chosen to live here. At one end of Alexander Drive was the impressive Quarter Bridge pub and hotel, and at the other end was the Masonic Lodge. What more could a man in his position need?

I should point out at this stage that neither Auntie Eva or Auntie Preston were actually my aunties. My only actual auntie on the island, Marilyn, doesn't like to be known as *'auntie'*. Family life is nothing if not confusing. Cronk Gennal is the house where my Mum and her sister grew up with my Grandad (although they were farmed off to boarding school for most of the year). Grandad married Auntie Eva (a distant relative of Ned Maddrell, the last ever native Manx speaker) and she moved in, along with her mother, Auntie Preston. There is no reason for you to know any of this, I just like to show off that I can still remember this part of my complex family tree.

Around half an hour's walk from the seafront, it was also a short meandering stroll from the other favourite place of my childhood - Nobles Park.

I had never seen anything like Nobles Park in England. It was a kind of holiday leisure park with numerous novelty outdoor sporting activities that any self-respecting young boy would have killed for the opportunity of a few hours play in its surrounds.

Situated behind the Grandstand, St Ninian's Church (I only recently found out that I am friends with the vicar there - hello John!) and Douglas Prison (I don't know anyone from there, but hello anyway!), it may be tucked away, but it is well worth a visit.

Without doubt it had the best Pitch and Putt course on the island. I once hit a score of 72, and wrote to tell all my friends back home. Yes, writing, it was like texting/e-mailing but slower. A testing course on which I spent many hours and days shanking, slicing and hooking whilst watching the boats come in.

When they closed that course, I seriously wanted to write to the City of Douglas

Corporation. One reason was that I wanted to tell them that they had a very silly name for a local council, the other was to tell them that the removal of the Pitch and Putt course had ruined my Summer holidays. I didn't though. It would have looked petty, and it would have indicated that I really didn't have much of a life to talk of.

Apparently they shut the course for *"Health and Safety"* reasons, as people from the neighbouring properties had complained about stray golf balls hitting their property - though I am guessing not the neighbours at the prison. Also they wanted to put in a service road to the campsite behind the Grandstand. Much like when our local council shut our village's school to build houses and then didn't have a school to send all the children from the families living in the new houses, I felt that possibly Douglas Corporation hadn't thought this through. Yes, the campsite would have marginally better access and more people would go, but where would all these extra people play Pitch and

Putt? I am guessing the provision of Pitch and Putt is no longer a consideration in the planning process, but I am sure you will agree, we are a poorer society for this.

Ah well, Nobles Park still has other attractions. A wonderful TT themed (more of this later) crazy golf course being the pick. Probably the best crazy golf course I had played in its day, but now slightly disappointing. Year on year, more and more of the course falls into disrepair. The big bridge with pool underneath used to be the best hole - I think it was meant to represent Ballaugh Bridge, though Ballaugh doesn't have a toddlers' swimming pool underneath it, as far as I can tell. First the paddling pool was filled in, then the bridge was removed.

The Gooseneck hole now has a goose that has lost its neck and head, probably making it illegal under The Trades Description Act, as well as deeply disturbing for children interacting with it. Kate's Cottage no longer has a cottage - it seems to have been left derelict - and Hillberry now has half the giant toadstools missing. All in all, underwhelming.

The putting course is now a children's play area. The aviary is now closed. Some of the tennis courts (though not all) turned into BMX track/skate parks. I am sure this appeals more to the youths of today, but for me it seems like a great loss and a missed opportunity.

But back to the Prom. If you wanted to travel from one end of the seafront to the other, during the height of Summer season, then you could take a horse drawn tram. Again these trams hark back to a bygone age but there is something reassuring about the *'clippety-clop'* sound echoing across the beach - possibly a less reassuring smell, but that's horses for you.

For those that worry about the mistreatment of horses, we are talking about big shire horses, who seem to enjoy pulling around an open-topped tram full of portly tourists. I don't speak horse, but I suspect they would say it is 'neigh problem' if asked.

It's not a bad life, and at the end of your long career you could be sure that you wouldn't end up in a Findus lasagne as someone kindly set up the Isle of Man Rest Home For Old Horses. This is where old work-horses go to retire - though I am not entirely sure about their tax and pension arrangements. You can visit the rest home, which is a short drive out of the city towards Castletown, and feed and pet these beautiful equine companions, if that is your thing.

The horse tram runs from the harbour at one end, down to Derby Castle at the other. The Derby Castle section, up towards Port Jack and Onchan, has seen better days. There remains the shell of two giant, once great, leisure development buildings. The first, *'Aqualand'*, used to house an Olympic sized indoor swimming pool - it has now been razed to the ground and is used as a car park for those that work in the city. The second,

'*Summerland*', has a more chequered and tragic history.

For me, Summerland was a pleasant (if tacky and slightly overpriced) entertainment complex for holidaying families. Think Butlins and you'd be pretty close. It originally opened in 1971, and was full of the usual distractions - restaurants, bars, cafes, pool tables (including a pretty exciting octagonal pool table, for no apparent reason) and a roller disco. There were plenty of arcade games too - we would save our pennies to play the now forgotten '*Rally X*' game, going from A to B as quickly as possible, with plumes of toxic smoke coming out the back. In fact it would be like a metaphor for many of my future journeys made in cheap and unreliable cars that I continue to make to the present day.

However Summerland held a dark past. In August 1973, a freak fire killed 50 people and seriously injured 80 more. Before the days of non-flammable building materials being commonplace, it was an accident waiting to happen. The asbestos lined buildings (no really) and bitumen/plastic covered ceilings meant that many people were unable to escape. There were many avoidable reasons for the fire claiming so many lives, but I won't go into them here. Summerland was fully rebuilt in 1978, a jaded version of its former self, and finally closed for the last time in 2005. It was at this point demolished and the site remains vacant.

Above Summerland there used to be two massive hoardings on the hillside in the style of the famous *'Hollywood'* sign in California, but both fairly anti-climatic. The first said *'Onchan Park'* - somewhere you will hear more about in the next chapter - and the second announced *'Electric Railway'*.

No horses here, this is Derby Castle, all aboard the Manx Electric Railway to Laxey...

3. Laxey

The Manx Electric Railway - or MER as it is commonly known - provides wonderful coastal views as it winds its way up the Eastern side of the island from Douglas all the way to Ramsey, 17 miles to the North of the capital.

When the line originally opened in 1893 the line was around half its current length with the trams terminating in Laxey, a 45 minute pootle along some of the most scenic parts of the Isle of Man, and that will be our destination today. However, with a railwayman father, I know you would be disappointed if I didn't give you the full guided tour of the line as we meander our way towards my favourite seaside resort.

The MER is the longest narrow gauge railway in Britain and its rolling stock is among the oldest in the world. Not in a really bad British Rail way, but in a harking back to the good old days of railway vintage kind of way.

The usual set up for the MER mainline would be a two tram coupling. One a lovely warm oak panelled covered tram where tourists can enjoy the journey inside the compartment with relative warmth and comfort, and the second a more rickety tram with open sides ensuring that all occupants get blown to bits before reaching their destination. I will let you guess which we would usually choose.

The open carriage was the only the choice for a family with a sense of adventure. The main aspect of the adventure being whether you would survive to spend a day at the beach, or whether you would succumb to pneumonia first. The sides of the tram could be rolled down to offer some protection from extreme conditions, but 'extreme' in a Manx sense would usually have had to involve sleet, snow, driving rain or locusts.

Also with the wooden sides of the tram rolled down, it would be impossible to see any of the views outside, which kind of defeats the whole purpose of going on the journey in the first place.

There are plenty of places to stop off on the way to Laxey. In the first few hundred yards of the journey, there used to be two more of the islands leisure parks. And, of course, by 'leisure parks' I mean like Nobles Park in the previous chapter and not like Alton Towers or Thorpe Park.

No rollercoasters to be seen here, but plenty of crazy golf, pitch and putt and other exciting distractions for people like me.

I think my holidays to the Isle of Man have made me something of a crazy golf addict. For me no trip to a British seaside resort is complete without a round of golf up a mountain or through a windmill. If I can jump off a bridge too, so much the better.

Onchan Park, perched on the hill above the now redundant Summerland complex, does not disappoint. Whilst I have to admit the crazy golf course isn't the best I've played, its tired features are rescued by the fact it is situated right next to the boating lake where many families like to relax by chugging around in circles. Introducing some jeopardy to the mundane is surely an inherent feature of crazy golf, or if it isn't, it should be.

Under-hit your ball and you won't get up the hill. Too hard and you may lose your ball in the water, or decapitate a small child. It's those elements of risk that really help to focus the mind.

But unlike Nobles, the management of Onchan Park clearly hold little truck with the political correct nanny state idea of Health and Safety. I wouldn't be surprised that if at least one of the staff there reads the Daily Mail too.

They have a pitch and putt course. Given the tiny size of it, two holes aside, it could be more accurately described as a putt and putt course. But they encourage you to live life on the edge - proper golf balls (not the soggy multi-coloured rubber variety that travel about 6ft before coming to a halt) and proper golf clubs - an 8 iron being the weapon of choice for the average punter. You can spend an entire day peppering the whole of the leisure complex with Dunlop 1s and 2s, and no-one ever has a bad word to say, not even the neighbours who seem to have accepted a long time ago that this good clean fun is probably preferable to an extended campsite with people talking and drinking in the early hours on their doorsteps.

Behind the cafe is a Go Karting track. Stock car races are regularly held here, but during the daylight hours of summer season the tourists are allowed to tear around in the park's very own Go Karts. Of course, there are safety instructions: *"Here is your helmet, here is your accelerator...try not to kill yourself."* Wise words.

The other leisure park slightly further up the MER line closed during the 1980s. White City was not, as it may sound, the venue for several World Cup football matches in 1966 or for major athletic sporting competitions such as those held in the 1948 London Olympics - but rather a decidedly tacky leisure park who's main focus seemed to be a small Go Karting track where you couldn't kill yourself at high speeds. We never bothered going to White City before it closed, which probably tells you all you need to know about how rubbish it must have been.

This section of track neighbours some of the most prime real estate opportunities on the island. Onchan Head is unrecognisable from how it was 30 years ago. On the site of the White City complex are a series of modern houses offering family living as well as executive holiday lets. Next door used to stand The Majestic hotel - one of the island's premier nightspots in the swinging 60s and one of the places my parents used to 'step out' when they were 'courting'. Again this has now been replaced by numerous expensive looking glass fronted holiday boltholes.

Opposite The Majestic was one of my parents' favourite restaurants, the very upmarket Boncompte's. Grandad and Auntie Eva would treat them to a rare slap up meal, whilst Auntie Preston looked after my sister and me at home. Boncompte's is now a Chinese restaurant, the other restaurants they would visit - The Crow's Nest in the crown of the Sea Terminal building and Jurgen's on Douglas sea front have also changed hands and closed many years since. On the upside they can now pop into KFC for a bargain bucket.

Undoubtedly modern tastes have changed. Whether it is the food you eat or the way you holiday, things have evolved.

Past The Majestic and around another couple of MER bends, the eagle eyed amongst you will spot that at the Howstrake stop the stone building, which looks remarkably like an old style bus shelter, says 'Howstrake Camp' on the back in giant painted letters. This style of sign is reminiscent of the old adverts you see painted on the side of old buildings in historic towns - you know the sort that advertises Oxo, Camp Coffee or Bile Beans and the like. This probably gives you an indication of the era this particular sign dates back to.

In around 1897, Howstrake became one of the first holiday camps in the world. Whilst this probably conjures up images of Gladys Pugh, Ted Bovis and Peggy Olrenshaw manically flitting between chalets with or without mop and xylophone, shouting *"Hi-di-hi!"*, the reality in the early days was very different.

For starters, the camps were all male affairs and secondly the accommodation was a series of tents rather than chalets. These two facts may or may not have contributed to the well-known phrase *"being as camp as a row of tents"*. Think more National Service chic, rather than 1950s ballroom glamour and knobbly knees competitions.

In 1937 however, a great storm of controversy was whipped up when the new owners looked to extend their consumer base by allowing women to holiday at the camp. I can imagine the po-faced moral indignation that this may have stoked amongst some of the tabloid press community at Fleet Street, but it is worth stating that the small number of women who could now attend (if they so wished) would now be housed in separate, segregated bungalow accommodation. I imagine chaperones may also have been in attendance and no sherries would have been served after 10pm lights out.

Requisitioned by the armed forces during the Second World War, Howstrake stumbled along during the tourist boom of the post war years but the writing was on the wall. By 1973 the camp had closed, and despite being sold a number of times to various different investors and companies the site remains derelict to this day. A haunting reminder of a bygone time.

Across the bay from Howstrake is Groudle Glen. A couple of twists up the MER track and you are there. The imposing Groudle

Glen Hotel a welcome retreat for those who like to walk the glens.

There are 18 National Glens on the Isle of Man, owned, run and maintained by the Manx Government for the Manx people - these are open to the public and offer a variety of views of the island's natural beauty. They also predominantly smell of garlic. Groudle is one of these.

What the glens have in common is that most offer peaceful forest walks, usually with rivers running through the middle and possibly a waterfall thrown in for good measure. Groudle also has a narrow gauge railway.

Like something out of the Thomas The Tank Engine books, Groudle Glen's railway is a short stretch of steam railway. It doesn't go far, but is a pleasant afternoon's entertainment for all the family. Trivia fans will know that Thomas is set in the fictional area of Sodor - what you may not know is that the Church of England Diocese that covers the Isle of Man (don't ask, it just does) is called Sodor and Man. Coincidence? I'll let you be the judge.

Created in the Victorian era (yes, did you guess?), the line used to take people from the Groudle interchange up to a zoo at Sea Lion Rocks. From 1896 to 1939, this was a major tourist attraction, however with the arrival of the Second World War and there being no tourists to make the zoo viable, it had to close. Rumour has it that rather than killing the animals the owner chose to release them into the surrounding area to fend for themselves. Numerous sightings of a polar bear in the waters around the headland at Groudle seem to back up this story, though no conclusive proof has ever been supplied to back up this theory. Nowadays, the journey up to Sea Lion Rocks will afford you views of nothing more exciting than some rocks which the sea lions used to sit on back in the day. Not quite the tourist draw it once was.

Not all the glens on the island are public. A few stops further up the MER is the Request Stop at Garwick Glen. An abandoned shelter all that remains to indicate that trams ever regularly stopped at this point in the journey. The glen has long since been privately owned. I've never been into Garwick Glen, I've only managed to steal a glance of what can be seen from the road, but I am told that the bay used to be a common place for smugglers to bring in contrabands and hide them in the many caves and coves sited on the beach. It's a mystical area and such stories of daring-do and cut-throat pirates add to the allure, even if they are not in the slightest bit true. It does however contain a small group of trees which randomly resemble a key from a great distance away, this is also passably interesting when there is little else to talk about.

Between Groudle and Garwick is the Liverpool Arms Hotel. It is known as 'The Halfway House' - this is because it is, as the name suggests, situated halfway between Douglas and Laxey. There are a couple of other halfway houses on the island, and they are worth keeping an eye out for, as they give you a good idea of how much longer you need to keep the kids entertained for. The Liverpool Arms is one of the few which is still a working pub, and it is well worth visiting for a lunchtime roast.

But onwards and upwards. From Garwick we remain inland for a couple of miles, following the road as it cuts through the farm land on the outskirts of Laxey. If you are visiting the beach, then you will want to get off before the main Laxey MER stop at South Cape. Or as the station sign helpfully says: *"South Cape - Alight here for the beach"*.

Don't gamble on a stop which does not tell you that you can alight there for the beach. The stop before is 'Fairy Cottage' and I imagine many confused guests from Howstrake may have got off here unintentionally with mindboggling consequences.

But South Cape is where we want to be. It takes a couple of minutes zigzagging your way down the hillside between the houses and public conveniences until you reach the seafront.

When we were small we would head straight for the outcrop of rocks on the right hand side of the beach. Laxey is a rocky beach full of stones and pebbles rather than lovely golden sand. If you are spending the day there, you will want to find somewhere comfortable to plonk your towel. Our little outcrop of rocks was situated in front of what used to be the only cafe on the small promenade, the appropriately named 'The End Cafe'. A small welcoming family business filled with garden benches, people wearing *"Frankie Says Relax"* t-shirts, whilst a young man out the back covered in grease worked on his beloved motorbike. It was the 1980s.

Sadly, as time moved on, the cafe closed. A giant mural painted on the side of the cliffs behind indicate that there used to be at least one other place for refreshments back in the day, a giant cat without a tail, advertising the 'Cat With No Tail Cafe' - the Manx are nothing if not imaginative when it comes to naming commercial ventures. But sadly, both these businesses had gone to the wall, in more ways than one looking at the mural.

Why did the cat have no tail, you ask? It wasn't brutality on the part of the owners, you understand, it is a reference to the famous breed of feline found on the island which has no tail. The Manx Cat, or 'Manxie', is alleged to have lost his tail when Noah was shutting the door to the ark back in the days of Genesis - the first book of the Bible, rather than Phil Collins and Peter Gabriel's rather disappointing soft rock outfit.

The story says that the pair of Manx cats were last to board, and as Noah slammed the door he accidentally caught their tails in it and ripped them off. Whilst I have no formal theological training, I have to express my doubts that this is accurate...but that's how the tale/tail goes.

Other cats have now come from the mainland onto the island (blooming foreigners coming over here taking our jobs and stealing our women!) so there is a wide variety in the length of cat tail. Some have no tail at all, some have a small stump, others a few inches, and a few have full length. Whilst the indigenous moggies do not seem too bothered about tail length when pairing off, they do seem to like their beaus to have fuzzy faces - as the old joke goes, this is because 9 out of 10 cats prefer whiskers.

In more recent years we have gravitated towards settling ourselves down at the other end of Laxey bay, nearest the harbour. A small cafe/shop has been set up next to the bus shelter and the concrete terracing at this point offers a flat floor to lay towels as well as some protection from the howling wind.

You may think that if it was a blowy day that you wouldn't even be out on the beach in such weather. However, you have to remember that this was not only our one Summer holiday of the year, it was our only holiday of the year, full stop. Therefore, rain or shine, we would be out on the seafront in our shorts and t-shirts, a good book (well, a paperback or puzzle book) and a set of playing cards. This was our one opportunity to sun bathe and get some sort of tan - whether we went red from the sun or the constant sandblasting from the gusts of wind swirling around the bay, we will never know. I have laid for hours and hours on this beach, pondering life and daydreaming about the future. The clank of the trams rattling over the tracks and the MER whistles blowing, mixed with the sound of seagulls, the only reminder that I was not on some South Pacific island somewhere but instead in the heart of the Irish Sea.

If you do venture as far as Laxey town itself, then there are a few sights worth seeing. At the MER station, the pub 'The Mine's Tavern' gives an indication of what might be on offer, but I can recite for you the history in full through the medium of song:

Laxey was a mining village many years ago,
There were 600 miners working under
Captain Rowe
The bottom of the mineshaft was below the
water line
So they had to build a wheel to pump the
water from the mine.

And the Laxey Wheel keeps turning, turning,
turning,
In Lady Isabella's memory,
And while the water flows
The Laxey Wheel still goes
And the Laxey river runs down to the sea.

For three quarters of a century there were
fortunes lost and found
As miners dug the lead and zinc from
underneath the ground,
Then came a great depression in 1929
And the miners drew their wages for the last
time at the mine

It's stood now for a 100 years through wind,
snow, rain and drought,
And it will keep on turning till the sands of
time run out,

And though the main mine building is no more than a shell
The Wheel still stands majestic in the shadow of Snaefell.

I know this song, by Stuart Slack, because my parents would record my sister and myself singing this into a tape recorder as children. We also sang a song about *"Ten Little Men In A Flying Saucer"*, but that seems less relevant at this particular juncture.

The Laxey Wheel (or 'Lady Isabella' as it is also known, named after the then Governor of the Isle of Man's wife) is the largest working water wheel in the world. As the song says, this wonderful piece of mechanical engineering was needed to raise lead and zinc from deep under the ground and it used to provide much needed employment for people all over the island. It has now been turned into a visitor attraction and you can climb to the top of the wheel. This will not only allow you spectacular views of this part of the island, but also ensure you are soaked to the skin by spray from the wheel as it continues to pump water from the hills.

You get to the wheel from the station by walking along 'Ham and Egg Terrace'. This street gets its name from the days when the miners used to come down here to get their breakfast before setting off for a hard day's graft at the coal face. A lot of time and effort, not to mention money, has been invested not only to maintain the wheel but also to restore some of the outer workings further up the valley. There are some lovely short walks available that let you see the remains of the pump house, the adit level and other areas which would have been bustling hives of industry in their pomp. You can also walk the first 100 yards or so into the mine and see the cramped conditions the miners had to work in, if you don't mind donning a hard hat.

On the other side of the station are the Laxey Woollen Mills. They still make various woollen clothing and tartans for those braving the Manx weather. The Isle of Man has its own tartans, the most famous being 'The Laxey Manx Tartan' incorporating *"the colours of the Island - purple to represent heather, blue for the skies, yellow for the Manx gorse, the green of the hills and the white of the clouds"*. There is no brown despite the amount of bulls**t generated in this marketing spiel.

If you were to get one of these tartans made for a kilt - say you were marrying a Scot and this was a deal-breaker on the whole getting married thing, for example - then it is helpfully listed in the tartan directories as an 'historic tartan'. What this means is that the shop can charge you twice as much to you for the honour of purchasing it.

I don't mean to belittle the fighting achievements of the Manx, but the Latin motto on the national flag *"Quocunque Jeceris Stabit"* which is said to mean *"whichever way you throw, it will stand"* is hardly accurate when you look at the history books. We may like to pretend that the Manx have fought throughout history to defend their borders from the Celts, Picts, Vikings, Angles, Saxons and so on and so forth but actually what the Manx have been very good at is adapting to newcomers, to such an extent that they perpetually managed not to be eradicated.

The Vikings are a great example of this. Whilst mere mention of these warriors in blonde pigtails make us think that everything in sight would have been raped and pillaged, the reality seems to have been very different. It seems that once a full blown invasion was launched, the Manx welcomed them in with open arms. The families inter-married. The names, cultures and languages were merged and new strong bonds of fraternity moulded. I am not saying this is a bad thing, not in the slightest, but it is hardly the foundations of a plot for the Manx version of Braveheart.

The Manx tartan is an amusing distraction for tourists and golfers to indulge in. Its heritage can be traced back to the 1950s invasion of the bucket and spade brigade, hardly 'historic'. Sure, wear it with pride, but don't think it gives you any cultural claims to centuries of defending your territories from the horrid oppressive world without.

On the upside, it does make a nice cosy kilt.

Come on everyone, back on the tram to Ramsey!

4. Ramsey

In 1899, six years after the Douglas to Laxey branch of the Manx Electric Railway line opened, the powers that be hit on the whizz-bang idea of extending the line even further up the east coast of the island to the small fishing town of Ramsey.

Actually, *"whizz bang"* isn't a particularly appropriate term when referring to the MER – *"pootle-clank"* may be a more apt description.

Although today it takes around 45 minutes on the tram to get from Laxey to Ramsey – in other words, nearly exactly as long as it takes to do the first section of track between Douglas and Laxey – there are two things that you need to know about the 9 miles of journey:

1) In contrast to the older section of track, there are few notable stops or landmarks to enjoy. In truth, it's pretty bleak unless you like looking at sheep grazing in fields – and if you do like to spend your leisure time eyeing up our woolly friends, we should probably pass your details to the Manx Constabulary,

just to be on the safe side. Dhoon Glen is a notable exception, but there are equally beautiful glens which are situated nearer to the capital, if that is your thing.

2) It's significantly colder than the Douglas to Laxey route. I put this down to the fact that Ramsey is further north and is therefore further from the Equator. In fact, I am sure this must be the reason.

Ramsey is the island's second biggest town, and still has a bustling working harbour.

There are at least three rather splendid pubs on the quayside which are worth a visit: The Stanley – a spit and sawdust type pub, definitely the sort of place you should go for a pint of stout, mild or a decent bitter is your thing (also, coincidently the pub where my Dad would spend many an hour of our holiday); The Mitre – a very posh looking old-school hotel set on many levels, with a wonderful restaurant bar with a panoramic view over the harbour, and a fantastic menu to match; and finally, further round the quayside into the main square, The George – a beautiful, friendly pub and the perfect place to sit outside with a cold refreshing glass of something when the sun is out (I also saw a particularly bizarre episode of Deal Or No Deal here on their big screen where Noel Edmonds was dressed as a mad scientist and the contestants styled as gruesome monsters, for no apparent reason. I will ever thank The George for engraving this onto my brain.)

If you are after a Manx beverage, then the obvious choice would be a pint of the local ale. There are two local brewers of note on the island – Bushy's and Okells (for the yokels). Both make their brews in accordance with "*ancient Manx purity laws*" which were laid down in around 1874.

Yes, I know 1874 is not *"ancient"* by most standards, but I guess it is all relative.

I should probably explain that *"Manx purity laws"* have nothing whatsoever to do with fair maidens wearing chastity belts to preserve their dignity, and refers rather to laws which forbid the use of any supplement to malt, hops, sugar, water and brewers' yeast. Although that thing with the maidens sounds more fun.

The beers have a distinctive taste. And *'distinctive'* is my euphemism of choice. Beer is not usually my cup of tea at the best of times – in fact, tea is my cup of tea at the best times – but if you like to try something a bit different then do give it a go.

If you prefer to imbibe something a bit harder, then the drink for you is probably Manx Spirit. Well, Manx Spirit tastes like whisky…but doesn't look like whisky (it is a colourless liquid like a vodka rather than oak coloured), and therefore is apparently not allowed to be called 'whisky'.

A High Court case in 1997 ruled that the spirit made at Glen Kella on the island could not describe itself as 'whisky' because despite coming from a single malt it had been redistilled and had lost its distinctive colour. It tastes good though.

Doing some research on this – including an extensive tasting process – I discovered that Manx Spirit, now called ManX (which sounds more like a dating site for identity protective males) describes itself as a *'whiskey'* on its website. I don't know if this helps skirt around a few legal loopholes, or whether a subsequent legal appeal has been held, but I do know that this particular description is doubtless incorrect. The single malt used to redistill Manx Spirit is from Scotland - and Scottish whisky is spelt with no 'e', it is the Irish variety that is spelt whiskey. It's a small distinction, but I still feel it necessary to air this particular grievance. It strikes me rather odd that the Manx ales have no 'e' numbers, but that the Manx Spirit can have 'e' letters.

If it's food you are looking for to accompany your alcoholic beverage – or should that be the other way around, with my family it's difficult to tell – then the food of choice should be fish based.

I now feel obliged to tell a story from when I was much younger and I picked up a queenie down at the harbour. (I am sure we have all done it in our youth and it's not something I feel ashamed of.)

Of course, queenies are small Manx scallops. Queen scallops are a fraction of the size of a traditional scallop but are probably tastier, softer and more succulent. They go very nicely in a cheesy mornay sauce, or with garlic butter or smoky bacon. Is your mouth watering already, or is it just mine?

When I was but a mere slip of a lad, we were walking by the dockside when the fishing boats were coming in after a long day trawling the Irish Sea, and a friendly old fisherman in oilskin and sou'wester, threw to me a shell from the pile he was boxing up to go to one of the many local seafood restaurants. It was a lovely ornate shell not too dissimilar in shape from the one you will be familiar with from a famous petrol station sign…no, not Esso, the other one…like those shells you used to see on people's mantelpieces in the 1970s, which individuals used to use as a stylish ashtray. (I will now wait for older readers to explain to younger readers 1) what a mantelpiece is 2) what an ashtray is.)

I thought little of this kind gesture and took it away with me to use when I would no doubt later in life embark on my own smoking career. But halfway through a game of pool at the local arcade this shell mysteriously opened and the poor creature inside mournfully stared back at us. It was like that moment in a film when you find out that the old lady you have seen throughout is actually the ghost of someone who died many years before. It's unlikely, unpredictable and makes you jump out of your skin, even though you are sure it can't do you any real harm.

When I say this creature from the deep stared back at us, I should clarify that I don't think it had any eyes. It was probably just trying to breathe. I know there is that old cliché about being a fish out of water, but it wasn't exactly gasping for air…which is a good thing considering we were in a very smoky snooker hall.

What we should have done was take the fish home with us and cook it for our tea – what we actually did was cry and cry until our parents took us down to the local pier to throw it back into the water. As the queenie plopped in, the shell slowly closed and it joyfully lollopped to the sea bed. A good thing was done that day. But seriously, do go out and eat some, they are lovely and probably not all as cute as that particular fella.

Other delicacies you could sample from the waters? Crabs, lobsters and other crustaceans are a fair bet for a tasty treat, but probably the most famous export is the Manx Kipper. As I am sure most of you know, a kipper is a variety of smoked and split herring. You can get them vacuum packed and sent to you in the post. (I am not making this up!) In our house there is always much debate about them.

The first bone of contention with the kipper is the…er…bones. I am not sure how such a delicious creation can contain so many tiny, throat stabbing bones, but I have always felt this was the herring getting its final revenge on anyone stupid enough to attempt swallowing it. I can't understand why God hasn't invented a series of animals for us to consume which are both juicy and tender, without the need for bones ruining the whole thing. Has he really thought this thing through?

The second problem is the smell. It isn't unpleasant, but it is lingering. The traditional way to cook a kipper is to place it in a pan with some butter, but the quicker more modern technique is to put it in the microwave for a couple of minutes. If you choose the latter option, you may as well just put your microwave in the bin afterwards. No amount of scrubbing or airing will expel the scent of kipper. It will be there for months when all else has been killed off, like the proverbial cockroach in a nuclear explosion.

In hundred years or so, the earth will be run by nuclear weapon wielding, kipper eating, cockroaches – just mark my words. Don't say you haven't been warned.

The final argument I have with my wife is over which is better: The world famous, delicious, best on the planet Manx kipper; or the inferior, less tasty and undoubtedly less satisfying Scottish kipper? I think we all know the answer to that question, it's just that some of us are unable to admit it to ourselves.

Something you could have to accompany your fish of choice is some fresh seaweed. It's much nicer than it sounds, and is farmed off the coast of the Isle of Man due to the cleanliness of the water in the Irish Sea. Yes, there is a booming trade in healthy and nourishing seaweed, much nicer than a packet of crisps or a bar of chocolate, I can tell you.

Aside from that you have a traditional array of farm produce to tickle your tastebuds. Sheep, cows, eggs etc all with a distinctive Manx taste. My favourite is the sausage. If you are staying in a local B&B, have the Full English breakfast, but don't call it the *"Full English"*, they are a bit funny about things like that.

But away from the dinner plate and back to Ramsey. A short walk from the harbour is the Mooragh Park. As you may have guessed, like Nobles Park and Onchan Park, this is one in a long line of fine leisure parks on the island.

The pitch and putt course disappeared even before my arrival on the island. It has now been transformed into a rugby pitch and BMX track. (Rather one end is a rugby pitch and the other is a BMX track, I can't imagine the two pastimes go hand in hand.) But there are other ways to while away the time.

There is a very good crazy golf course. There is a broad TT-lite theme to it, but unlike Nobles Park, no effort has been made to pretend each of these holes bears some resemblance to a specific part of the Isle of Man. Rather the holes are constructed to look like they are being played up, over and through a series of mountains. It is more

James Bond in its inspiration than anything Manx. The sides of the course have been marked in places with black and white kerbs to indicate this might be a racetrack, but in truth the links are tenuous at best. Half the course is on grass rather than concrete (though the obstacles are made of stone) and in the middle of the course lies a mini cannon. There is no obvious explanation for the cannon, and it is not a part of the course in its strictest sense. Maybe if Alan Sugar was here he would turn to it and say *"You're Fired!"*? Yes, that could give it some comic purpose and potential not currently afforded to it.

Across the path from the crazy golf is the island's premier putting green. 18 holes (rare that parks bother with doing a full course, in my experience) and the site of many a hole in one whoop and holler. Next to this a quality crown green bowls rink.

I've always thought I'd quite like to take up crown green bowling, I probably would if it attracted a younger clientele than that which currently frequents this sport. As Northern pastimes go, it is far preferable to pigeon fancying, whippet racing or pipe smoking. It is a relaxing game, with no small element of skill involved. Still frustrates me that you can work hard to craft a winning opportunity and then someone can tank their last bowl as hard as they can to scatter all your handiwork and steal an unlikely point. But then, I suppose the ends justify the means.

There are three tennis courts which have seen many an epic Cross family encounter. Most sets over the years have been edged 6-4 against my parents, almost as if they were trying to let me win. From a very young age we would bring our own tennis racquets with us. This seemed to make sense when we were very small, as very few places would stock plastic racquets and sponge balls, but even into my teens I would bring over a couple of racquets and a set of balls so we could have a proper game. This may seem excessive for a two week summer holiday, but given that the racquets the good burghers at the Mooragh Park provided to players were made of wood, you can understand our thinking.

Next to the tennis courts at one end, in a smaller court that resembled a giant cage, were motorized kiddies cars. I can remember a red and blue one that resembled space ships (like Thunderbird 2, for those that remember). They were powered by diesel and made a heck of a noise and smell. When we were small, me and my sister would spend long periods driving round in circles, chasing each other. We would never actually catch one another though as the cars went at exactly the same (slow) speed. I was saddened when the kiddies cars disappeared (apparently stored in a shed, as they were not being cost efficient), but even more horrified when they reappeared years later, concreted into ground in the cage. Who wants to sit sedentary in a spaceship car that doesn't move? It was almost like not only had they killed this once great beast, they had then decided to display it publicly to discourage anyone from making any future such errors. They should have pulled out the entrails and hung this up next to them, whilst the cars themselves were thoughtfully displayed in a gibbet.

At the other end of the tennis courts is a small children's play park. The usual array of swings, slides and play equipment exists as on most parks, but I can clearly remember that half way up the hill (towards where the grand Ramsey town houses overlook the Mooragh Park) there being a giant rainbow slide. You used to climb up these slippy wooden steps and then race to the bottom of the rainbow in a hessian sack. I am sure I didn't imagine this, but can't imagine why you would need a wooden staircase to climb into a rainbow and then what a hessian sack might represent in this geological scene. I am not saying it wasn't fun, I am just suggesting that somebody hadn't thought the narrative through.

Running alongside the length of the park, sandwiched between the play areas listed above and the sea front, is a massive lake. My sister would go canoeing in here most holidays, although she never progressed to a level good enough to enable her to appear on the 80s show *"Paddles Up"*, which I am sure still narcs her to this very day. Most other people on the lake, aside from families rowing (and when I say "rowing" you can interpret that word however you wish, both meanings are accurate), would be scout and guide types whose parents had clearly decided that the best way to fill in the long summer months would be to go on an adventure course. This is fine, but I prefer my adventures to be a little more challenging than whether I might contract Weil's disease or a urinary infection. There was a small island (about 12 feet by 20 feet) that people would disembark upon and spend literally seconds looking for buried treasure and conch shells before finding tenuous reasoning for murdering their friends or, more often than not, getting back into their canoe looking deflated and disappointed.

Ah, Ramsey, you little tease.

My Grandad clearly had a soft spot for Ramsey too. He had a second home there. A lovely town house off Parliament Square. It was sold long before I came on the scene, but my Mum tells me how they used to spend their Summer months there as children. I've never fully understood this, I mean, I know Ramsey is a lovely enough place, but if you are going to buy a second home, why buy one a few miles up the road on the same island? It's not my idea of a holiday getaway. Nowadays you'd purchase somewhere in the South of France or in rural Spain, but back in the day clearly the well to do of their time used to enjoy staying in a home from home where you could pretty much also still see your first home, if there wasn't a giant mountain in the way. Grandad probably had more money than sense. He was an optician, he made a good living. Not so sure about how his customers felt....in fact he probably saw them coming.

But look at me with my East Coast obsession. Anyone would think there was nothing of interest over to the West of the island...

5. Peel

If Laxey was always my beach of choice, then Peel would always be my sister's.

Most people would see Peel as a more conventional choice too. No rocks to be seen here, just vast expanses of golden sand as far as the eye can see.

If the postcards are to be believed, this is where everyone comes to lie on the beach, take donkey rides and pose in their speedos. Of course, the reality is very different.

Most of the postcards on display date back to the 1970s – a time when being pictured in public next to a donkey in your speedos wouldn't get you arrested and added to some kind of register.

If you were to make the journey today then you'd be lucky to see a handful of people wrestling with windbreaks and dodging dog turds while playing beach tennis with the kids.

But let's take a moment to consider the journey and what sights can be seen on the way.

Over in the West of the island, Peel does not have the luxury of trams or trains linking it to the capital, Douglas. If you are relying on public transport (which let's face it, is never entirely wise), then it's the bus for you.

Douglas bus station is conveniently situated next to the sea port. (Convenient if you are getting off the boat, not that convenient if you are going anywhere else.) A bus to Peel would take you around 40 minutes.

One of my favourite spots on the ride way out West is the ruins at St Trinian's near Marown, at the foot of the Greeba Mountain.

I should point out that this is not the site of an old school which was burnt down by pigtail sporting, stocking wearing, hockey stick waving schoolgirls but rather an old church which is said to be haunted.

Yes, haunted. By a buggane.

Bugganes are reportedly evil spirits. Imagine a cross between an ogre, a witch, a mole and that guy with the big hat from Time Team and you are getting close.

They are not allowed on hallowed ground (probably something to do with an ASBO obtained by the Church, but this particular fact is not clear) and therefore, when this evil spirit possessed the church that was being built at St Trinian's, a buggane was keen that no roof would be put on it – that way no service could take place to make the building sacred. Clearly the Manx Government of the time had not thought about introducing a bedroom tax, which would have been far more effective in evicting an unwanted tenant.

So every time that they put a roof on the building, that evening the buggane would appear and smash the roof into tiny pieces so no service could take place.

And so along comes Tim the Tailor. Being a poor down on his luck sew and sew (see what I did there?), he makes a bet with his friends that he can stay in the church throughout the evening following the roof being put on.

Either Tim is very brave or very stupid. Perhaps he thought that there was no buggane (not an unreasonable assumption) and that perhaps it was some elaborate ruse by the local building community to extract maximum payment from a gullible local vicar? Either way, he finds himself in the building that evening when to his horror a big angry buggane appears through the floor and, in no uncertain terms, tells him to buzz off.

Tim jumps out of a window – which fortunately has also not been put in – and he runs as fast as he can back down the Douglas Road towards Marown. The buggane smashes the roof to the floor and gives chase for about a mile or so until Tim reaches Marown Church. Standing on hallowed ground, the buggane cannot reach him. Apparently so annoyed is the buggane by this, he throws his head at the Church and it explodes into flames. Where there is blame there is a claim and all that, but I'd like to see such an incident go to court so the full facts could be ascertained.

No idea how Tim the Tailor managed to outrun a magical evil spirit but I bet by the end of it he had a stitch.

Anyway, that's the story of why St Trinian's no longer has a roof and remains abandoned. I have visited the building just once in all my years visiting the Isle of Man. I was about 12 and I remember the experience to this day. Whilst we were nervously looking through a window, a white rabbit hopped up to us looking menacing. We looked away, and then when we looked back it had turned into a black rabbit! I have no idea what the significance of such a change is, but apparently bugganes can change shape and form – that is why we don't see them nowadays because they are disguised as humans. Perhaps they are not as skilled when it comes to rabbits and they sometimes get the colour wrong. (Either that or there were simply two rabbits, but I think that unlikely.)

Further up the road is the town of St Johns, this has its own dark history in Manx folklore. Towering over St Johns is the heavily wooded hill Slieau Whallian. Apparently Slieau Whallian is where people suspected of being witches were taken to be tried and executed.

The name Slieau Whallian translates into English as *"Whelp's Mountain"*, and if you were taken here back in the day then you would have had a dog of a day.

Firstly the suspect would be thrown in the river or swamp at the bottom of the hill. If they died then the good news was they were not a witch, but the bad news was they were dead.

If alive, they would then be taken to the top of the hill and put inside a barrel with spikes inside it – the barrel would then be rolled to the bottom of the hill. If you died, you were not a witch – in fact you were probably very holy/holey.

If you survived being smashed up against trees in a spiked barrel, you would then be taken out and burnt alive at the stake. It seems witches can't survive fire – which rather begs the question why they bothered with all the other stuff.

But it would be wrong to say that this is all St Johns has to offer. Indeed it is at the very heart of Manx democracy. The Manx Parliament, or Tynwald, has sat here for many centuries. The earliest record of a

Tynwald on the island dates back to 1417, but it is thought that they existed here since the 8th Century, though not at this exact site.

Whilst the roots of this fledgling democracy lay with the old Norse kings and their Viking chums, nowadays its processes are well established. Indeed this is one of the oldest established Parliaments on the planet.

There are two branches to Tynwald – the House of Keys and the Legislative Council – most of their work takes place behind closed doors, inside buildings which have roofs (probably to keep the bugganes out) – but once a year, on 5th July, Tynwald sits in the open air here at St Johns.

Tynwald Day is a great national occasion with great pageantry and tradition. It is a time to pass laws, but also to celebrate the Manx identity. Think of it as an equivalent to St Patrick's Day for the Irish, St David's Day for the Welsh, St Andrew's Day for the Scots or St George's Day for the English, but with less fighting.

There are usually representatives from the Royal family and the Church of England present, but don't let that put you off.

Also behind Tynwald Hill is a lovely craft centre, so if you do get bored, you could always pop in.

But onwards to Peel and the smell of kippers. Straight ahead of you on the road to Peel you will see an old tower on the horizon. This is known as Corrin's Folly. Keep heading towards it and you will eventually reach Peel.

Corrin's Folly was built in 1806 by Thomas Corrin – and this is where his family are buried. You can still visit the tower today, it is a short (but hilly) walk up from Peel Harbour up Peel Hill, although it is not possible to get inside the folly at the current time. It's a great view, but there is no café.

Peel itself is an old fishing town and houses one of the biggest smoking facilities on the island – I'm not talking cigarettes, cigars and pipes here, but rather a building that smokes herring. The smell is distinctive and not unpleasant.

One of the first buildings you will see on the quay next to the smoking factory (again, not the smoking factory you are initially thinking of – please see above), is the House of Manannan.

Manannan mac Lir was the first ruler of the Isle of Man and a son of a sea god. You can tell already that perhaps, in fact, neither of these statements is 100% true. He is a character from legend who protects the Isle of Man from invaders.

I once had a sweatshirt that had a picture of him that said *"A legend in his own time"* – although he is actually a legend in whatever time you choose to look at him. Also his head broke the middle of the statement, so most people read the top to say *"A leg end in his own time"*. Even then, something was a foot.

When you look at the history of the Isle of Man, Manannan hasn't done that well on protecting the island from invaders – whether it be the Vikings, the Irish, the English, the Scots or the Welsh, the attacks have been nothing if not frequent. However his most famous act of 'protection' is when he puts his cloak around the island so people cannot see it.

His *'cloak'* in this metaphor is the Manx sea mists – hiding your island in amongst sea mist is the sort of thing you can do as the son of a sea deity – but nowadays he only tends to do it to make it difficult for the Queen to arrive. Many say this is to do with Manannan wanting to underline that the Manx are not the subjects of the UK – others say this is to do with the weather being bloody awful.

Whilst Manannan's cloak can no longer hide the fact that the Island is there, it can sometimes make it difficult for airplanes to land so maybe there is a grain of truth in it.

The House of Manannan is not where this man of myth used to live, rather it is a museum which looks at Manx history. The museum is simply fantastic and I would recommend it as a great day out for all the family.

There is a good mix of interactive exhibits and a wide range of subject matter. Everything from the Stone Age, to the Vikings, to the modern day fishermen is covered here. It's interesting and accessible and you'll need to give yourself a few hours to see the whole thing – and you will want to see the whole thing. (For me it is much better than The Manx Museum in Douglas – but that too is also worth a visit on a rainy day, of which there will be many.)

If you come out of the House of Manannan and walk down the harbour side towards the sea front, there are a number of good local hostelries. Probably the pick of these is The Creek Inn, which serves good food and drink – including a fine array of fresh seafood – and is well worth sticking your head into.

On the left hand side of the bay, when you get to the front itself, is an old breakwater and behind this a much bigger pier. If you want to go fishing then I can recommend the pier. Sit on the top and pray you catch a mackerel or coley fish rather than something bigger, or you could find yourself getting dragged in.

I remember falling off the small breakwater when I was about 7 years old, I was accidentally pushed in by a bigger boy whilst fishing for small fish with a net, and managed to swim back to safety. It made me never want to do that off the pier, because I imagine it would hurt a lot more.

We used to go to Peel to watch the seals. This is one of the places they like to come and swim – and no doubt take easy pickings from the fishing vessels as they come home of an evening. You also get basking sharks.

Basking sharks are very large creatures and usually hit the headlines in the Summer when (lazy) newspaper reporters write stories about people off the coasts of the British Isles being *'terrorised'* by sharks. Conjuring up images of Jaws may sell papers but it is worth noting that basking sharks live off gulping large amounts of water and sifting krill through their gills rather than eating humans. I guess they could suck you to death, but why would they want to?

A little known fact, but a true fact (as opposed to all the other ones you get in this book), is that Olivia Newton-John is a big supporter of the basking shark and is President of the Isle of Man Basking Shark Society. She's got chills, they're multiplying, and she's losing control. That will be the icy cold Irish Sea for you.

On the headland behind the pier are the magnificent ruins of Peel Castle. The castle itself is actually situated on St Patrick's Isle but this island is now connected by road by a causeway to the mainland.

Peel Castle was built in the 11th Century by Viking ruler King Magnus Barelegs (I bet he got chilly at night). It remained a working fort until the 18th Century.

Nowadays the castle is an open-air museum. Manannan mac Lir is your guide – clearly the cloak shrouding work is drying up – and you listen to a commentary through a handset relating facts to you about the objects/buildings you are standing in front of.

My dad always told us about the story of the Moddey Dhoo, a mysterious big black dog which haunted the castle, prowling around and pouncing upon helpless victims at night. I don't know what it did to the soldiers garrisoned there, but the thought of it used to keep me awake as a child.

"Don't go out at night, you may get eaten by the Moddey Dhoo….Aaaagh!" You get the idea.

The castle always made me think of the 1980s children's show *'Knightmare'*. That's the kind of setting you have to picture. Though the many open-air performances of Shakespeare I have seen within these walls are far more frightening than Treguard could ever conjure up.

Anyway, that's enough about Peel, do have an ice cream on the front though, you've deserved it.

Spellcasting…*D-I-S-M-I-S-S!*

6. Castletown

Douglas hasn't always been the capital of the Isle of Man, up until 1869 that honour lay with Castletown – and as the name suggests, it is a town with a castle. Good work everyone on that particular naming committee.

Situated in the South of the island, Castletown is under an hour away by bus from Douglas – however you can take a steam train which would get you there in about 40 minutes.

The original steam train line ran from Port Erin to Douglas and opened in 1874. There were also routes from Douglas to Peel and Ramsey but these no longer exist.

The station, including café and ticket office, in Douglas is deeply impressive in all its Victorian splendour. If you want to travel the 8 miles in style to Castletown, this is the route for you. All smoke and whistles as you rattle through the countryside through idyllic areas like Santon.

We rarely did the train journey due to the cost. It was not part of the British Rail network and therefore we did not get our 100% discount on travel. I am sure it's much better now, but old habits die hard.

I am far more familiar with the bus route. Heading out past Quarterbridge, past the Pulrose golf course, the views soon become the usual mix of fields and farmland – but there are a few sites of interest on the way.

There used to be a haunted former hotel that lay in ruins to the right hand side of the road – in recent years the site has been completely transformed. The new Mount Murray Hotel is an imposing 4 star hotel and country club with its own 18 hole championship golf course to boot. The evil spirits haunting the ruins were clearly told to 'buggane' off. It's very nice and has great gym facilities.

On the opposite side of the road is a course where people practise for motorbike trials. If you remember Junior Kick Start with Peter Purves on BBC during the Summer holidays, this is the type of riding I am referring to. In fact many of the top riders on Kick Start came from the Isle of Man – though not that one who whacked his goolies on the balance beam and made the St John's Ambulancemen fall head over heels into a pit full of straw. If you want a bunny hop and a balance on top of a stationary car, these are your boys.

Slightly further up is the Isle of Man Cat Sanctuary. I know many people like to visit to see the animals there, but we once had cause to call in when we found a tiny kitten abandoned in undergrowth near Groudle. The poor thing was covered in fleas and hadn't eaten for days. We wrapped it in a towel and took it straight away to the Sanctuary. It was one of the lucky ones, sadly many kittens are abandoned, mistreated or killed by their owners before they ever have a hope of being adopted by someone who actually cares for them.

The village of Santon is where my aunt Marilyn used to live, before she moved to the centre of Castletown – you can still see her old cottage where the road forks just after the Motel. My Uncle Ian has family buried in the graveyard nearby. It might be a small community but it means a lot to us.

And Santon is your last chance to turn around before the Fairy Bridge.

The Fairy Bridge is a bridge which straddles the main road between Castletown and Douglas. It is said that if you do not say hello to the fairies as you cross the bridge then bad luck will befall you.

This may seem like errant nonsense, but many people, including my Mum would without fail say *"Good morning, Little People"* or *"Good evening, Little People"* as we crossed.

'Little People' is the name which people give to fairies on the Isle of Man because as we all know, fairies do not like being called *'fairies'*. It is a well-trodden Manx euphemism, as is *'long-tailed fella'* when referring to a rat. If you hear either of these phrases, you now know what they refer to.

If you ignore a fairy, or worse mock them, then it is said bad luck will befall you. The bridge is situated in a dark section of road where the ground is substantially lower than that on either side – indeed the section of road on the Castletown side of the dip is a notorious accident black spot* (*more on this phenomenon later) called *"The Black Boards"* where many have lost their lives – so you'd have to be pretty brave to deliberately tempt fate in this manner.

Many people not only respect and fear the fairies, they love them. On one side of a road is a tree covered in messages from small children asking for wishes to be granted by the fairies.

Whilst you may want to encourage your own children to join in, there are three very good reasons not to do this: 1) You might get run over by traffic, 2) Folklore seems to suggest that these fairies are malevolent creatures who punish bad people rather than reward good ones, 3) This Fairy Bridge is in no way magical and does not have any fairies living beneath it.

Hopefully that hasn't disappointed too many children reading this Chapter, but in case it has, I should probably say that the reason for clarifying this last point is that the real Fairy Bridge is some miles away, off the beaten track. This is because the fairies don't like being disturbed by traffic or well-wishers, so they like to keep their real location a secret. What a relief.

Before Castletown itself, the road reaches a roundabout with three legs. Yes, even the roundabouts are Manx over here. This is the small town of Ballasalla.

Ballasalla may seem to be a small settlement of little note, situated next door to Ronaldsway Airport, but with a little investigation there is plenty of adventure to be had.

Rushen Abbey is just off the main street in Ballasalla and has been turned into a museum chronicling the life and works of the island's community of Cistercian monks.

We often forget the role that monks had in educating society, as well as keeping records of significant historical events, on top of their duties devoted to spiritual reflection and the welfare of the wider community.

The monks served an important purpose as a kind of middle man to the power-wielders at the castle down the road from where the then capital took its name. They also had a distinct advantage that most ordinary folk did not have – they could read.

The Abbey was founded in 1134 by King Olaf I. A good Viking name, for a good Viking King. It remained an important religious and cultural centre right up until the mid-16th Century when the monastery and church were dissolved by Henry VIII. (Rushen Abbey shouldn't take this snub personally, Henry liked dissolving a vast array of monasteries when he wasn't chopping off the heads of various wives. It was like a hobby. If he had been ruling today he probably would have taken up polo instead.)

The monks gave us one particularly historically significant document, *"The Chronicles of the Kings of Mann and the Isles"* – a medieval Latin manuscript outlining the early history of the Isle of Man. Not sure why they did this, but perhaps it was out of habit. You can still view this document in the British Library in London – if that's your idea of a good time.

After the site fell into disrepair, it was acquired by Manx National Heritage in 1998 and since then a great deal of restoration has occurred. Graves of many of the monks were found throughout the site during this work, and these locations are helpfully marked by a picture of a dead monk. Unfortunately they did not live abbey-ly ever after.

In 1350 the monks built a bridge to cross the river so they could get their produce more easily to the North of the island. It is unclear whether this is what killed them, but for arguments sake we will say that it wasn't.

This bridge used to be the starting point of our walk to the other great attraction in Ballasalla – Silverdale Glen. If you do go by foot it is a picturesque walk through the glen following the Silver Burn river that all the family can enjoy/endure.

On the way you will not only see the bridge the monks built but also a well-used by the monks. OK, it doesn't sound that great, but it is something to pass the time on a dull Sunday afternoon. After a short stroll, you come out at Silverdale itself.

There is a restaurant, a craft centre and an all-important café on the site, but it is the grounds themselves that will keep bringing you back for more.

Outside the front of the buildings is a Victorian style boating lake. Take a row boat (or a pedalo, if you want to recreate the heady buzz of a week's holiday in Ibiza without the booze and terrible music) or watch the ducks as they paddle merrily with their ducklings.

There will not be many yellow ducklings though, as the seagulls tend to eat these fluffy little darlings first. I've seen this happen with my own eyes and it wasn't pretty. (It was a bit like that scene in Bambi where his mum dies, but imagine Bambi then getting swallowed by a giant seagull and you will be closer to what actually happened. Surreal and disturbing.)

There are two large children's playgrounds alongside with the usual combination of swings, slides, seesaws and springy things that don't really resemble anything in the human world. But the piece de resistance is the ornately carved Victorian roundabout.

I have a picture, one from every year of my life, of myself (usually accompanied by my sister) on top of one of these brightly coloured horses on the roundabout, as we ride round in perfect circles. It was probably quite cute when we were kids, but as you pass your 30th birthday and you still pose for a shot of yourself hanging on for dear life, screaming like a loon, it probably sends out a different message to those watching.

The roundabout is powered by a massive waterwheel next to the ride (though nowhere near as big as the Lady Isabella), and its speed is controlled by a lever. These buildings used to be a mill in their original form and the river helped to power their machines which cut and chopped the wood. I can only guess that this would have been the original purpose of the waterwheel, though a pleasant turn of the century ride for well to do families is equally charming.

My early memories of the café development are somewhat different to those people experience today as they sup tea and lick ice creams. Upstairs was a mini amusement arcade. I can remember both Rally X and Double Dragon featuring, so it must have been a pretty good one. Up a small flight of stairs in a very dark room was a single pool table.

But downstairs was where the real dark heart of this operation lay.

When I was small you could pay to go into a grotto. This sounds quite twee, but it was the most sinister grotto I have ever ventured into.

Normally a grotto would have a woodland scene, with elves jovially slapping each other's backs whilst Father Christmas readies his sleigh. What this grotto had was a woodland scene, with the dwarves from Snow White and the Seven Dwarves being brutally oppressed by a slave master buggane. Imagine if Disney Land did a chamber of horrors and you would be close to picturing the dystopian world that someone at Silverdale had imagined would be good for youngsters to spend their pennies on.

Sometimes when I go to sleep, I can still see the big yellow eyes of the buggane staring out like extras from that Bonnie Tyler video as a Dopey, Bashful and Sleepy are whipped for below minimum wage earnings to create wooden products for the public to enjoy. Anyway, I suppose the mill owners had to make a living, and who would complain if they were likely to get an exploding buggane head thrown at them? Exactly. Best not to dwell too much on such thoughts.

But onward and outward towards Castletown itself. Past the airport on the outskirts of town and into the harbour. Actually, best to go around the harbour or you'll get a bit wet.

During the Summer season this is where the famous/infamous bathtub races take place. In Peel you may get Viking longboat races, but in Castletown you get bathtub racing – it's the sporting equivalent of having someone throw wet sponges at a man in stocks at the village fete, so all in all we should not take it too seriously – but clearly there is more chance of drowning with this pastime.

On the harbour side is the wonderful Glue Pot pub. Officially named the Castle Arms Hotel, it is a lovely old style snug and one of the oldest inns on the island. There are worse places to spend an afternoon's contemplation, regardless of whether people are trying to submerge themselves in bathroom furniture in the bay or not.

However as this grand old pub is situated a short stumble from the police station, you may want to choose another spot for your late night revelry.

From the Glue Pot, Castletown is your oyster…or your queenie…or whatever the appropriate Manx shellfish of choice is for this metaphor. I am pretty sure it isn't a kipper though. No, Castletown is very refined, a cultural, political and historical hub rather than a grimy parochial fishing town of old. As if to emphasise this point, directly opposite the Glue Pot is Castle Rushen which for centuries was the seat of power for the Lords of Mann.

Castle Rushen predates Health and Safety legislation as well as the Disability Discrimination Act so isn't the most accessible if you want to go to all areas to see the rooms, armouries and battlements but it is well worth a visit. We never went in to the castle as children as my Mum couldn't stand spiral staircases – which is something of a standard in old castles – but as a teenager it was a fantastic adventure for us. We would squeeze through tight spaces, look at instruments of torture and hang off the slippy roofs – basically do anything that may endanger life and limb, safe in the knowledge our Mum would not be on hand to tell us off.

Do you want to know an interesting fact about spiral staircases inside British castles? You don't? Ah, that's a shame. Perhaps you should skip down a couple of paragraphs in that case, because the rest of us are about to do some proper learning – by which I mean I am going to subject you to another pointless bit of knowledge that even a half decent pub quiz wouldn't bother you with.

One interesting thing you will notice about the vast majority of spiral staircases in British castles is that they spiral clockwise. The reason for this is that this gave the advantage to soldiers protecting the castle. Back in the day, all soldiers would be taught to fight holding their swords in their right hands – even if they were left handed. This meant, by having a clockwise spiral, those soldiers protecting the castle could come down the stairs whacking the intruders freely, whilst those coming up the stairs couldn't reach their foes as the central wall of the staircase would obstruct their attempted blows. Clever construction.

Castle Rushen is probably most famous, in the Isle of Man if nowhere else, to be where great Manx hero Illiam Dhone was locked away as a political prisoner by the Lord of Mann, the Earl of Derby.

Illiam Dhone, or William Christian to give his English name (the name literally translates as 'Brown William' from the Manx), led the Manx Rebellion of 1651.

James Stanley, the 7th Earl of Derby, had gone to fight with Charles I in an ill-fated campaign against Oliver Cromwell and his Roundheads in England. I am sure most of us are more than familiar with this particular piece of history, but as my wife is constantly telling us that they didn't learn about the English Civil War in schools in Scotland, it bears the briefest recap.

To cut a long story short, and apologies to any history scholars out there who actually care about this sort of thing, King Charles I was in dispute with Parliament. Basically he felt he was right about everything and that Parliament shouldn't interfere with his God given right to do whatever he wanted. The elected representatives in Parliament felt slightly differently and objected to little foibles of Charles such as bursting into Parliament and killing MPs he disagreed with. Battle ensued between the King's supporters (the Cavaliers) and Parliament's supporters (the Roundheads) – and eventually, Cromwell was victorious.

The sum total of this messy period of division and civil war was that King Charles I was executed – as were many of his supporters – and Oliver Cromwell became Lord Protector and had a song written about him by Monty Python.

So back to James Stanley. Captured by the Parliamentarians, it was all looking a bit bleak. Actually, considering he was captured just outside Crewe, it was probably looking very bleak indeed. His wife (still on the Isle of Man on account of being a woman) struck upon the genius plan of getting her husband released by offering the Isle of Man to the Parliamentarians in exchange.

This was fatally flawed for a couple of reasons. 1) She hadn't consulted the Manx people about whether they might want this to happen, and 2) the Parliamentarians executed her husband anyway.

The Earl of Derby wasn't particularly popular on the island at this time, partly because of laws he had passed that affected the farming community – and partly because his wife had just attempted to sell them all down the Irish Sea for her sweetheart.

Illiam Dhone was already a man of position having been appointed as Receiver General and he was a natural choice to lead the revolt, seizing many of the island forts. The rebels then entered into their own negotiations with the Parliamentarian forces, which was rather pragmatic in the circumstances.

Two years later, and with Mann back under the control of the new Earl of Derby, Charles Stanley, Dhone was accused of misappropriating money and put on trial for various offences. I am sure Charles Stanley, the 8th Earl of Derby, was simply acting in the interests of justice, rather than settling old scores and petty vengeances – he simply did what any son who had lost his father to a random beheading might have done.

Dhone was taken up the road to Hango Hill and shot by a firing squad.

Only ruins remain today on Hango Hill, but it will be always keenly remembered. Not least because, when we were small, my sister found a £5 note on this site. So, yes, some ancient Manx hero was executed here, but we gained £5 to spend on sweets. Swings and roundabouts.

A short walk from Castle Rushen are two more museums. The Nautical Museum is probably quite grandly titled given that it is essentially a tour around the house of Manx privateer and man of mystery George Quayle.

When we say *'privateer'* in this context we euphemistically mean a smuggler. If he had been lower class we might have said *'pirate'*, but a gentleman of the seas by nature of his birth gets a grander title. Perhaps he had a hand in naming the museum? (Given that he had been dead around 120 years before it opened, I would suggest the evidence is in his favour on that one.)

A small vaguely interesting house, only really worth the entrance fee to see the secret entrance into his hidden boathouse under the main building.

The Old House of Keys doesn't even have that to its credit. Situated roughly between The Nautical Museum and Castle Rushen (directly next to the police station), it is an impressive room but not much more than that.

This was where the directly elected lower house of the Manx Parliament sat. Until 1706 The House of Keys convened in Castle Rushen itself, but subsequently this building opposite was erected for this purpose and here it stayed till around 1874.

If you imagine how a glorified Parish Council Chamber may look, then you'd pretty much have the nail on the head here – and I say that as a former Parish Council member.

Even today the new House of Keys only has 24 members, but it sits in Douglas next to the

Government offices known as *"The Wedding Cake"* – named due to its distinctive shape and the fact that they knew it would all end in tiers.

This building is a reminder of a bygone age, but not in a healthy *"Let's climb the battlements"* kind of way, more a *"Let's find the secret snuff box"* kind of way. Stuffy, fusty and only of limited appeal to the political geek. Suffice it to say, I love it.

But enough time has been spent here in Castletown, it is time to head down to the deep South…

7. The South

We're going to the deep South, island style. Already you are probably imagining yokels on banjos, with an inexplicable fondness for dungarees. In reality nothing could be further from the truth - no, they don't play banjos in this part of the world.

Actually the two main towns in the very South of the island are quaint seaside affairs, with the usual attractions of promenade, pub and...places to park your car.

Port Erin and Port St Mary wouldn't be our first choice for a beach day (see chapters on Laxey and Peel), but if the weather was bad, it was likely that we would end up heading beyond Castletown and down towards the tail end of the island in search of sun. If that was the case then Erin would be our next port of call - the unfailing logic, as ever, being that this town would be bound to have better weather due to it being much closer to the Equator than the rest of the island. It's hard to argue with such wisdom, it should apply in all circumstances, wherever possible.

Port Erin is around 15 miles South East of Douglas, but only a 10 minute drive from Castletown which is a leisurely 4.5 miles down the road - so hardly inaccessible. As well as being at the end of the historic steam train line, there are regular buses and good road access too.

Given its title, you may (wrongly) presume that the town gets its name from its association with the Irish mainland, but actually the name is derived from the Manx for *'iron port'* or *'the lord's port'*. The Lord's Port sounds like a great name for seafront pub, but so far the local hostelries have resisted the temptation

If you can resist the temptation of the local hostelries, there are other things to enjoy in Port Erin. The iron port is sheltered by two towering headlands, which help to protect the town from being battered too much by the combination of strong winds and the Irish Sea - on the most southerly of these, Bradda Head, sits a distinctive tower.

The Milner Tower, like Corrin's Folly in Peel, was never a residence, rather it was built as a commemorative tower to mark and pay tribute to the works of local philanthropist William Milner.

It is an odd construction, but beautifully odd - like Lily Cole or Sophie Dahl, you know it shouldn't be attractive but it's the imperfections and uniqueness that give it its charm, and you can't tear yourself away from the sheer beauty. In fact, the building looks a bit like someone has dropped a giant key and lock onto the cliff edge. This is no coincidence. William Milner built his fortune as a locksmith and safe-maker of great renown - the design of this tower is a humorous and loving tip of the hat to the work he did while he was still alive.

The tower was built in 1871 and is still accessible to this day. You used to be able to drive your car all the way up Bradda Head to the foot of the Milner Tower, but erosion and the passing of time have meant that vehicular access is now prohibited. It is, however, still possible to walk up to the tower. If you park your car at the Bradda Cafe, there are a choice of two leisurely walks up to the headland. The Coronation Footpath is the most gentle of these, taking a fairly direct route across the flatter high-ground - there is also a more challenging walk which is nearer to the sea and starts off going downhill from the cafe, but steeply rises as you near the tower. Both walks take between 10 and 15 minutes and have beautiful views of the bay and surrounding area.

Amongst the lobster pots and fishing boats, if you look carefully, you will also see an abandoned lido tucked into the rocks - it's odd to see it simply left to its own devices, but there is not much call for such things nowadays. It had latterly been used as a fish hatchery and farm for oysters, turbot and lobsters - and had been taken over in its final state as a marine biology research station for the University of Liverpool - but since 2006 it has been simply allowed to fester. You would have to be very brave to want to take a dip in it now, that is all I would say!

When you reach the headland's summit, you can clamber up the rocky foundations and enter into the tower itself. Whilst the inner rooms are locked or boarded up, if you go up the spiral staircase to the very top you come out on a small viewing platform. It's a bracing and invigorating experience due to the exposure to high winds, but it is well worth doing - just make sure you wear a jumper.

Around 100 yards to the South of the Tower is an old pill box gun emplacement, which I presume like most examples on the island, dates back to the time of the Second World War, when members of the Home Guard would attempt to pick off passing German airplanes. (No doubt, someone would attempt to do this whilst shouting *"Don't panic, don't panic!"* at a balding overweight Captain in an unconvincing wig, if we are to believe everything we have seen of the Home Guard on film.) This gun emplacement has a small plaque outside which marks it out as being the site of the Kodak World Photo of the Year. Yes, C. W. Powell's photo of the Milner Tower, taken from the pill box, was as good as it got during the immediate post war period - a truly golden age.

On the opposite headland, there is not much of note. However half way up you can see Mull House, the property where former Formula 1 World Champion Nigel Mansell lived for many years.

You can say what you like about racing drivers wanting to protect their vast wealth by leaving the mainland to go and live somewhere with less aggressive/fair tax laws, but at least with Mansell he shunned Monaco and other such exotic locations to go and live in the middle of the rain-lashed Irish sea. That is genuine commitment. Indeed, he is well-loved on the Isle of Man, having involved himself in island life at every level rather than cutting himself off. He became a Special Constable with the local constabulary too. Can you imagine being pulled over by him and being asked if you think you are Michael Schumacher? It must be surreal.

Anyway, I'm giving the great man the benefit of the doubt here...though reading recent press reports I see he has just opened a motor museum with his son in, that other well-known tax haven, Jersey. So who knows. At least he didn't go totally tonto and open an organic buffalo farm like Jody Scheckter.

Just over a mile down the road is the much prettier, but much quieter, town of Port St Mary. Like its neighbour, it is accessible by train, bus and car.

The town takes its name from the ancient Chapel of St Mary, which has long since gone. There is far less to do in Port St Mary, but it is picturesque and often has holiday clubs on the beach during the Summer which bring the whole place to life. We rarely went to Port St Mary when we were younger, as there was something of a run-down feel to it - the broken, over-turned, raft in the middle of the bay seemed to symbolise this most aptly, though there is an RNLI boat permanently moored in the harbour, so you can't say they weren't prepared if someone had decided to give the raft a go.

Only on reaching adulthood did we spend more time in Port St Mary. A fine selection of pub restaurants selling fresh seafood being the main draw, though there was one memorable occasion when I took my dad on over the 9 hole links course at Port St Mary Golf Club. Memorable as I do not think I have seen such a poor array of shots ever chosen, nor such amount of inventive bad language used in one half round of golf in my life. Other groups teeing off were playing for £100 a hole, we probably paid around the same in fees for lost balls.

Incidentally, Port St Mary's most famous past resident is arguably Molly Sugden from Are You Being Served Fame. I should say at this juncture that there is no museum paying tribute to the late Mrs Slocombe's memory and no building or memorial erected in her honour. It's probably safe to say though that over the years many of the locals would have stroked her pussy.

A mile further down the coast road from Port St Mary is the remote farming village of Cregneash. The settlement has been kept as a *'living museum'* to how life would have been on the island during the 1800s. You will be pleased to learn that Ye Olde Tea Shoppe does have electricity and essential modern things like kettles though.

Cregneash opened as a museum in 1938 and faithfully represents how life was for a small Manx rural fishing and farming community. Some of the thatched cottages have been sold off to private investors, but there are strict rules governing what can and can't be done to properties, in order to preserve the feel of the community.

As well as farming and fishing, the main employment for villagers back in the day would have been weaving or knitting. At Cregneash the museum workers put on national dress, weave, knit and perform duties such as blacksmithery using traditional methods - some even attempt to speak Manx. I am sure this is all great for the tourists, but it is a bygone age, and things have (rightly) moved on. Sure, acknowledge the importance of the rare four-horned Loaghtan sheep and traditional thatched roofs, but accept that community life has evolved and progressed for the better.

I have no problems with celebrating our shared national heritage, but unbridled nationalism and national festivals which celebrate how great things were in the past (when poverty was rife and life expectancy was low) leave me scratching my head. Do they think the old red phone box on the edge of the village is authentic Victoriana? Do they think Queen Victoria was Manx?...I don't know the answer to these questions, but I know they make a nice cream tea.

A short walk round the corner from Cregneash is my favourite location on the Isle of Man. Remote, peaceful and desolate, The Sound might seem like a strange choice for a day trip, but there is something mystical, raw and visceral about it.

Whenever I have needed to get away, I have come to The Sound and read a book, or done a crossword, and have just sat and let the world pass me by. It feels like the end of the earth, but in a very Manx way. I suppose The Sound is the Manx equivalent of England's Land's End.

Across the water, a short distance, from The Sound are a number of small islands. This outcrop was formed, as legend would have it, when Manannan mac Lir once got into a fight. (That is what happens when you go out for a couple of drinks at the pub, even if you are a sea deity.) Whether that is true or not - and let's face it, it isn't - what we have left behind is a small but beautifully formed archipelago.

The tiny group of islands include places such as Kitterland, Yn Burroo and The Stack but the biggest island by far, standing at around 1 mile across and long, is the Calf of Man.

The Calf of Man derives it's name from the Old Norse word *'kalfr'* which means a small island lying near a larger one, and not from any reference to being the back end of someone's leg. Privately owned till 1939, the Calf was donated to Manx National Heritage to become a bird sanctuary.

Now if you were to ordinarily say that you were going to a local beauty spot to see some choughs and possibly a shag, then you might expect to get arrested - but in the Isle of Man these are the names of two of the local birds you can see. And by 'birds', I mean the feathered variety. There is a Manx Shearwater colony and everything.

You can still visit the Calf of Man and its bird observatory and regular boat trips are available from Port Erin. Two things they do not tell you on this trip are as follows: 1) The most famous bird to come from the island used to be a Manx raven kept at The Tower of London - the Manx people are very proud of the service that it gave to the British monarchy and its body is now buried in the grounds of the tower. However this bird never visited the Calf of Man, so has now been written out of this particular ornithological history. 2) Manx birds of prey like the peregrine, merlin and hen harrier love to pick off more docile members of the bird community who are resident here. Again, this is something that is rarely mentioned - though it is something you can regularly see, if you are into that kind of thing.

Of course, death is a common occurrence in all walks of life, not just amongst birds. There are many ship wrecks lying at the bottom of the sea between The Sound and The Calf of Man that will attest to this. Two memorial stones lie in place at The Sound commemorating the worst of these disasters - one to the 1852 Brig Lily Disaster and one to the 1858 French Schooner the Jeune St Charles. The Jeune St Charles pays testimony to the bravery of local fishermen who went to the aid of those perishing in the treacherous waters and is in the shape of a giant white cross - constructed in 3D so that the cross is visible from all sides, it is called The Thousla Cross as this is the name of the islet it used to reside on to act as a beacon to other ships in this channel of water, but it was subsequently resited and is much easier to view today. The small plaque to the Brig Lily marks a tragic tale. Not only were some of the crew lost in the initial sinking, but also 4 local men guarding the vessel died the next day when the gunpowder in the hull of the ship ignited causing a massive explosion. There are 4 lighthouses in this small outcrop of islands that are still functioning today - as a sailor, it remains a place that you'd want to give a wide berth to.

It's not just bird colonies you can see here. There is a large seal colony too. I'm not sure why, but there is something I find incredibly relaxing watching seals. When they aren't fighting and maiming each other, they seem fairly placid sorts. In the water, they glide and duck, bob and drift, like an elegant balletic swan. Out of the water they sun themselves and groan endlessly, like an English family holidaying in Marbella. As I have never seen a basking shark at this part of the island, I can only presume that the seal is it's mortal enemy and it chooses to avoid it like the plague for fear of retribution - either that, or they just don't come down here. One or the other.

You can watch all these fun and games from a state of the art Visitor Centre at The Sound. There is a small exhibition section, which is rather underwhelming, but the real attraction is the cafe with its panoramic views of the Calf and surrounding seas. Whilst being a very modern development, the cafe does at least attempt to be eco-friendly and merge with its environment as much as possible - it is built into the headland and has grass turf on the roof, for example - which its much maligned predecessor did not. A big white monstrosity, the previous cafe - or *'hut'* as we should describe it - was extremely poor, in the wrong place and damaged natural features underneath it, which have since been restored. It also had giant white and red stone mushrooms for children to play on. I don't know if there are health and safety concerns with giant mushrooms, but I do know there should have been objections on grounds of taste.

So The Sound, nothing but happy memories for me...if you don't count the time we borrowed Auntie Eva's car to visit it and then on the way home a rogue stone knocked out the fuel line and we nearly blew up a small section of road on the main A5 road from Castletown to Douglas. Who knew that petrol tanks on old Audis could contain so much petrol?...Ah yes, totally blissful.

God bless the Beautiful South.*

(*And all other Paul Heaton bands.)

8. The North

It's only fair if we are going to focus on the South of the island that we also spare a few lines to talk about the North too.

Sadly the North, no matter where you are in the world, seems to have an unfair reputation as being something of a backwater where no good can ever come. I am reminded by Christopher Ecclestone's response as Doctor Who all those years ago when cockney chirptress Billie Piper remarked with incredulity: *"If you are an alien, how come you sound like you are from the North?"* His response?

"Lots of planets have a North". The same of course is true of most islands.

It is unfair to suggest that there isn't anything of particular note North of Ramsey - I get frustrated enough when those of a certain mindset suggest there is nothing of worth North of Watford, and whilst I accept in a footballing sense this may be true, I think culturally and geographically we have to argue otherwise. Having said that, when I looked at a map of the area North of Ramsey, someone had written on in large letters: *"There Be Dragons"*. So you'll have to make your own minds up.

The Northern most tip of the island is a fairly remote location called Point of Ayre. If The Sound is a Manx Land's End, then the Point of Ayre is John O'Groats. In fairness, if I had to choose to do a sponsored bike ride for charity, I would probably pick The Sound to Point of Ayre over Land's End to John O'Groats - whilst I could pretend it was because of the unique views, I readily accept it is because it is around 800 miles shorter.

The early indicators as you approach Point of Ayre are not overly welcoming. It may only be five and a half miles North of Ramsey but in many senses it is a world away. On your left hand side as you approach is a giant landfill site where seagulls gorge themselves on everything from rotting carcasses to rotting vegetables. You could be forgiven, given the smell, that this might be some clever chemical revenge attack on the UK by the Manx Government for all the damage that Sellafield is alleged to have done to the island over the years. (Not that anyone on the island calls it *'Sellafield'*, it is far more likely to be described as *'Windscale'* or *'that bloody thing'*.)

As you approach Point of Ayre itself, there are no *"Welcome to Point of Ayre - the Northern most settlement in the Isle of Man - your last pub was in Ramsey!"* that are so beloved on the mainland. I would not be surprised if the civic committee that came up with such ideas was chaired by the same man who came up with the *"You don't have to be mad to work here - but it helps!"* slogan. He was probably wearing a Homer Simpson tie at the same time too. No, no such hilarity and forced bon homie here - just a bunch of signs telling you to keep out because this is private property.

The only building at Point of Ayre itself is the lighthouse. This is where you would go if you wanted to watch the Isle of Man ferry going back and forth to Belfast from Douglas, but now it is strictly off limits, so instead you need to take a hard right at the signs and head down to the rocky beach below.

I can't blame the port authorities for selling the Point of Ayre lighthouse, or the family that bought it. These things go for millions of pounds nowadays as people look for quirky character homes with a sea view. Of course, if I ever owned such a property, I would spend most of the time pretending that I was starring in the Australian children's comedy *'Round The Twist'* - so it is best that it is put to better use.

You can get a Coach Trip to Point of Ayre or take the bus from Ramsey, but no trains or trams run this far up the coast. There is no cafe or other form of distraction on offer, so if you are seeking entertainment, this is not the place for you.

If you tire of watching the boats go by, you can take a short walk and marvel at one of the truly bizarre mechanical engineering feats of the 1920s, a concrete ship. Yes, you did read that right, a ship made of concrete.

I would love to have been in the meeting where that particular idea was pitched:

"You see boss, the price of steel is very expensive following the First World War, and for that reason we are going to make our next ship out of concrete! It's much cheaper!"

"What?! Will it actually float?!"

"Er, yes, I am sure it will."

"OK then, let's go for it....incidentally why did you say 'the First World War', don't you mean the Great War?"

"Er, yes, I did. Forget I mentioned it."

But float they did. The main problem about concrete ships was not their seaworthiness, but rather that their weight and shape made them less economic than conventional vessels, often outweighing the cost benefit of using concrete rather than steel in the first place.

This particular ship was called the Burscough and was built in 1921 in Preston, Lancashire. She had a length of 124 feet, beam of 23 feet, and gross tonnage of 299 tonnes - so a fair old structure - and ironically this would prove to be her unique selling point when her sailing days were over.

When the ship's owner could no longer make a profit from sailing her across the Irish Sea, she was deliberately run aground at Point of

Ayre to create a semi-permanent pier. If they had been pitching the idea on Dragon's Den I suspect that they wouldn't have talked about this *'multifunctionality'* and rather pretended that the entire thing was a wheeze to save on construction time at the site - build your pier in advance, let it sail itself across and simply plonk it where you want it. I like it, but can you run me through the numbers in your business plan again? Thanks.

Looking at the figures though, such a business plan - no matter how crazy on the surface - would be hard to argue with on a financial level. The Burscough was reported to have cost £30,000 to build as a boat but was sold for a scrap value of £250,000 as a makeshift pier. You do the maths.

But it's best we head back down the road. If we head in any other direction, we'll get our feet wet and catch our death, so Southward it is.

Whilst I want to do my best to sell this part of the island to you (metaphorically not literally), I do feel that the Manx authorities could do us a favour and employ officers every couple of miles to simply say *"Nothing to see here, move along"* and wave people onto the next village.

Having said that, we once got lost on these roads and nearly bumped into a giant hare. I have no idea how they breed them so big but it was like a GM version of Watership Down, scary is not the word. Not that that is the oddest thing you might meet on a lazy afternoon drive, wallabies are regular visitors. Apparently a pair of these cuddly marsupials escaped from the Curraghs Wildlife Park in the 1960s and now the Isle of Man has the largest Red Necked Wallaby population in the entire Northern Hemisphere, with a giant feral colony traipsing the North of the island! (I am just grateful that zoo keeper in Groudle only released the one polar bear, or we'd all be in trouble now.)

Even the main settlements here sound folksy and nondescript. Bride, with its beautifully picturesque church, sounds like it is a wedding venue for well-to-do couples. Andreas just sounds like a hairdresser's. It's not somewhere you'd want to spend any longer than you had to.

However there have been some residents here who have had little choice about how long they remained. During The Second World War the Isle of Man was used as the primary site for the internment of non-desirables. Whilst there had been a couple of small scale internment/concentration camps on the island in the First World War, they were adopted on a massive scale second time around.

Essentially, the UK decided that anyone who might be an enemy alien - male or female, adult or child, UK or non UK national - should be locked away for the duration of the war, safely away from the UK itself. What could be better than a small island in the middle of the Irish Sea? I often think when British politicians nowadays spout forth about holding all immigrants and asylum seekers on an island away from the British mainland, till we can decide if they are trustworthy and/or good for our economy, I wonder if this is the model that they are subconsciously harking back to?

Whilst the camps were policed by gun wielding soldiers and surrounded by barbed wire, many were located in some of the island's most desirable locations - for example, guest houses in Douglas, Peel, Port Erin, Port St Mary and Ramsey were commandeered. Although it is probably true to say they were chosen for their remoteness rather than their wonderful sea views.

It says something for the UK Government that they saw threats everywhere - even where there were none. Like Ronald Reagan with his *'reds under the beds'* attitude in the 1980s, there might have been a sense of unease in more liberal quarters - but having already lived through one World War and the thought of a possible German invasion increasingly real, the internment camp idea was actually very popular.

So who exactly were the British authorities scared of? Looking through the list of internees in the Isle of Man, across the 10 camps, it is a mix of those people who really might not have loved the Nazis. The poets, the musicians, the writers, the artists, the Jews, the scientists, the academics and the intellectuals. In short, this was predominantly all the people who were no longer welcome in Germany and had tried to escape the persecution in their midsts.

I doubt these people fleeing terror at home expected a particularly warm reception in the hands of *'the enemy'*, but what the Isle of Man ended up with were a group of centre left thinkers and doers much more keen to educate and liberate the lives of those around them than start a violent revolution from within.

The internment camps soon became places where artistic and academic abilities were nurtured and encouraged to flourish - indeed some of the paintings and writings were sold on to those outside for profit. Stories and cultures were shared and lasting friendships made. I particular like the story, though possibly apocryphal, that the Jewish internees were so taken with eating the Manx staple of smoked fish that they referred to it as *"Yum Kipper"*.

Low-risk internees were allowed to work on farms on the island and to go on excursions such as for walks or to swim in the sea - but essential liberties and freedoms were denied. At its height, in 1940, over 10,000 people were detained against their will on the Isle of Man. That number dropped as the war went on but that hole was soon filled by groups of Prisoners of War by the end of the conflict.

The only prisoners you are likely to see nowadays are those detained at Her Majesty's Pleasure - one such prison has been built on the site of the old Jurby airfield.

During the Second World War, Jurby was an RAF airbase. Predominantly used for various training exercises, the airfield was also used to allow Allied forces to run sorties protecting the cities of Liverpool and Belfast. Following the end of the war, the base was stood down, but is still owned by the Manx Government. Once a year an airshow is held, and regular bike and go-karting races are held in the intervening period, but aside from those interested by the appeal of a short prison stay, there is one Manx institution that must be visited - Jurby Junk.

Jurby Junk began on the airfield in 1972 selling second hand goods and antiques at rock bottom prices. The owner, Stella Pixton, says that she never intended to devote her life to this enterprise but, on leaving the civil service in London, had gone into business with her son to give him gainful employment.

41 years later and a combination of the passion shown by local residents and interest from visitors from overseas, has meant that she has never looked back.

Originally housed in the airfield armoury - which looked like a bunch of ramshackle industrial warehouses - these were demolished in 1994 and replaced with state of the art buildings. The rent is three times as much, moans Pixton, but I am sure she more than makes that back given the level of business this grand old venture still attracts.

Whilst most second hand stores of this sort might talk up the antiques side of the business, selling on high end products purchased at various auctions around the British Isles, the most popular part of this business with the general public are the endless aisles of books, novelty items and low end market pleasers. If you want a furry bookmark, a novelty mug or a humorous t-shirt, this is the place for you. Literally hours of fun to be had.

Whilst I don't fit into this above category, I always used to love a record shop. Jurby Junk allows me to indulge this part of my psyche, as I can flick through racks and racks of books that ordinarily I would never want to buy, but inexplicably walk away with a book of nonsense verse by Spike Milligan or Edward Lear and think I have had a really productive day.

Growing up with an unusual Christian name, it was also rare - if not impossible - for me to ever find a t-shirt or mug or any other item with my name on it. Jurby Junk was the closest I ever got to realising this dream, when I purchased a ceramic name plate for my bedroom door that simply said: *"Kerry"*.

It was only later that it was pointed out to me that the name plate had clearly been designed for a girl, with its painted picture of a lioness on the cover and pastel motif. *"Don't bring your gender stereotyping here"*, I thought, carefully trying to disguise the fact that I should have opted for the more manly plate with *"Ron"* the elephant on the front with bold black embossment.

At time of writing, I notice that Pixton has just put Jurby Junk up for sale. If you have a spare £80,000 for the 3,000 ft junk shop or the same amount for the similar sized bookshop, the next generation of the dream could be yours to enjoy.

No doubt, given the expected sales of this book, at the very least I could afford to buy a new name plate for my bedroom.

9. The Isle of Man Steampacket Football Festival

There are many reasons to travel to the Isle of Man. For us it was a good opportunity to visit relatives, but we always used to try and time our holidays to coincide with the Isle of Man Steampacket Football Festival.

The Isle of Man Steampacket Football Festival was an international football tournament held on the Isle of Man (rather than on the back of a ferry in the Irish Sea, as the name might suggest) which ran for a week at the start of August.

The event was sponsored by the Isle of Man Steampacket Company and I imagine that they may have had some say in the marketing, looking at the teams that were invited in the early years.

The real pull would be the lower league English football clubs - in those days it would be teams like Oldham, Bury, Stoke, Preston

North End and so forth - but invitations were also extended to professional teams from Scotland, Wales and Northern Ireland too. In fact, from those areas directly neighbouring the Isle of Man. It was almost as if the Tourist Board had a cunning plan to boost visitor numbers.

Part of the exclusive sponsorship deal would be that the football teams themselves would get free travel across on the Isle of Man ferry and put up in one of the island's hotels. Again, the idea for this being that fans of the club in question would then pay to go on the ferry and stay in the same hotels.

Having witnessed a fair few of these ferry rides, it really was something to behold. Professional footballers more used to travelling around in Bentleys or BMWs spending a four hour trip hunched over a toilet being sick, whilst crazy super fans of their respective clubs ask for autographs. Grown men sneaking off from their coach chaperones to have a couple of cheeky pints in the ferry bar. You get the picture.

On one occasion, we were flying in from Luton Airport (a choice which I am sure Lorraine Chase would have approved of, though sadly there was no Campari on hand to soothe our spirits) and one team had taken an executive decision not to take the ferry ride but instead take a plane and try to charge this back to the Isle of Man Steampacket. Unsurprisingly, the Steampacket were rumoured to not be overly enamoured with this, given that this was their one unique selling point which would also help to keep costs down. The team in question was Luton Town. Joe Kinnear - a man of few words and not one to run away from a situation he can tackle head on - was the manager at the time and was loudly making the point to organisers of the tournament that as his local team had an airport in the same town it would have been ridiculous to ask them to travel half the country to take a rickety old ferry. Not an unreasonable point, but not one that my family would have seen the merits of for obvious reasons. The moral of this story is always read the fine print of the contract before agreeing to anything.

The other team taking part in the tournament, without fail, was the Manx National Football Team. (Yes, there really is such a thing.)

The Isle of Man Steampacket Festival was one of the few tournaments that the Isle of Man national team would consistently qualify for. Some say this was due to the fact that this was a tournament they helped to arrange and would automatically qualify for as host nation, but this would be unfair - they also qualified regularly for the biennial Island Games, due to the fact they were an island. Aside from that, nothing.

In fairness to the Isle of Man national team, it would be impossible for them to qualify for a major tournament - partly because the pool of players they would be able to choose from would be tiny, and partly because they are registered and classified as part of the English FA rather than a national side in their own right. It seems odd to me that the Isle of Man would be registered *'English'* rather than have an arrangement like the Channel Islands do where any player (if of sufficient quality) could choose to either play for the Channel Islands, England, France, Scotland, Northern Ireland or Wales. Geographically it would make more sense too.

But these players for the Manx team were unlikely to reach those heights. Perpetually humiliated by their superior opposition, the local fans (and those supporters on the island watching matches their own team were not involved in) would cheer and scream enthusiastically more through hope than in any belief that they would win, in much the same way eternal optimists might have cheered for the Christians up against in the lions in the Coliseum.

The Manx national team was chosen not from people who were necessarily Manx nationals but rather from people who played in the local Sunday league. A couple of these players would go on to secure trials or short term contracts with mainland teams (normally teams which had played against them in this pre-season friendly).

More interesting were the old stagers who would turn up unexpectedly for a game. Two names immediately spring to mind. Firstly Rob Wakenshaw - a name only bettered for northerness in the Manx team by that of Albert 'Arrison, though I was always hopeful a Stanley Ollerenshaw would one day come out of the woodwork for a first cap. Wakenshaw had a handful of appearances for Everton in the 1980s, mainly as a substitute. From there he played for Carlisle, Doncaster (on loan) Rochdale and Crewe, before dropping into non league.

Wakenshaw might have been a journeyman professional in his day, who showed glimpses of brilliance, but for the Manxies (as absolutely no-one on the island calls them) he was a flair player. A Rolls Royce in a team of Trabants. He also looked a bit like the 80s wrestler Ric Flair, which was useful, if entirely coincidental - a mop of Boris Johnson like unruly blonde hair, at a time before anyone knew who Boris Johnson was.

He would inspire the Manx national side to some of its greatest ever results - a series of narrow losses and a memorable 1-1 draw against Wrexham at Peel FC. I was there and it lingers long in the memory.

Wakenshaw was a forward or winger by trade, but in his latter years, well beyond his prime, he would meander around the Manx midfield in a wandering free role, managing and bossing affairs from the centre of the park. The legs may have gone but the brain was still ticking. It was his wand of a right foot that arrowed the ball past the Wrexham stopper and sent the crowd into ecstasy that night - cars streamed through Douglas town centre beeping their horns and waving flags, and Manx Radio had extended coverage for the next week on most of its shows.

Beating Wrexham may not seem like a major achievement, but Wrexham were one of the few teams who would take the tournament seriously.

Pre-season tournaments are notoriously poor affairs to watch as a fan. Teams are concentrating far more on getting players fit and ready for the start of the season, rather than putting on a good display - this means that they are likely to have done several long runs and a variety of fitness routines rather than worked on some clever game-plan to break down the opposition. Watching professional teams running bare foot down Douglas beach, like a bad recreation of Chariots of Fire would always make me think of *Jossy's Giants* (Sid Waddell's remarkably accurate take of *"former player makes good by making children wear bin liners before social services can intervene and managing them to success"* for children's TV) and think that someone was bound to get a bit of glass in their foot and miss the bus to the game, with hilarious consequences.

You also get the feeling that the manager is trying to give everyone a game, rather than putting out a side that will blaze a trail through League Two next year. There is a Sunday league friendly feel, with coaching staff desperately trying to calculate exactly how many minutes John has to be on the park before coming off to ensure every player gets two-thirds of the game on the pitch. Rolling subs, no bookings, rush goalie, next goal's the winner.

There are also a large number of triallists - players currently out of contract, desperately trying to get someone to take them on on a temporary basis, which is unlikely as they have normally been released by their former club for not being good enough.

I always thought I could have played for the Manx national team. I used to play at a county standard and in non league for a time and my Mum was Manx. Sadly being good at football, or being Manx, were not qualifying factors - you had to have played in the island's Sunday league, they were adamant about this. I therefore asked John Rudge, then manager of Port Vale, for the chance of a trial with them in this tournament - but sadly the letter came back as follows:

"Dear Cronk, thank you for your interest, unfortunately we only take players on trial that have been identified by our extensive scouting network. Best of luck with your future endeavours."

Whilst I am delighted, and grateful, that John Rudge took the time to personally respond to me, I would have felt better if he had addressed me by my own name rather than my Auntie's house name. But that's the way it goes, it was not to be. (I always think it was their loss as much as mine, given that that *'extensive scouting system'* hadn't really done much for them in the past aside from rescuing Ian Bogie from his time at Leyton

Orient.)

Wrexham though were different. They realised that this was their one realistic chance of silverware in the season and you got the feeling they had prepared solely with the hope of lifting this title. Most seasons they were successful, reaching the final at the Douglas Bowl, if not winning the tournament outright. Hundreds of Wrexham fans would come over every year to roar their side to victory - they were fanatical, and the stories of rioting and central Douglas bars being trashed following defeats were not unknown in the Isle of Man Examiner's front and back pages.

One man alone would carry the burden of delivering victory for Wrexham. Talismanic frontman Karl Connolly - or as we called him *'The Weasel'*. A gifted, hardworking centre forward, yes - but also one that looked like a moany ginger weasel. It was unfortunate, but not unexpected banter.

Connolly started his football career at Napoli - that's Napoli in the Liverpool Sunday League, rather than the Italian top flight club of the same name - and was signed thanks to Wrexham's *extensive scouting system* of watching pub football in the Welsh and Liverpool areas in the hope of unearthing gold in them there hills.

Signed by long-serving Wrexham boss Brian Flynn, he was moved to play in the central attacking role following the departure of Gary Bennett to Tranmere Rovers in 1995 - off the back of him starring for Wrexham against Tranmere in the Isle of Man Steampacket Festival that year. Connolly went on to score 88 goals in 358 league games, but it is unlikely he would have crossed your radar. In the Isle of Man however his performances attained mythical status. The sponsors would never announce who the Player of the Tournament was until the day after the final had been played - a bizarre move meaning most of the players and fans were already off the island by this point - but this vow of silence could be corrupted, with the organisers often telling fans at the final: *"I am sure you could guess who it will be"* with a tap of the finger against the side of their nose. Nudge nudge, wink wink, say no more - Karl has scored 9 goals again, including one in the final, we know what you're getting at, your secret is safe.

So a battling draw against the tournament favourites, was always going to be an epic achievement for the Manx.

It would be much later in the history of the tournament, long after Wakenshaw had properly retired from football to concentrate on his cleaning business, that a new star would come on to the horizon.

Rick Holden - footballing swagger merchant, gifted wing genius, and top flight footballer of some renown - was minding his own business when fate came knocking. Or rather Peel FC came knocking. After a glittering football career - that started at Burnley,

Halifax and Watford, he moved up to the top echelons of the British game at Oldham and Manchester City, before finishing his career at Blackpool - he had hung up his boots and moved to the Isle of Man to concentrate on being a physiotherapist, heading up the Outpatient Physiotherapy Department at Nobles Hospital.

Holden was astute, realising there was life after professional football and had studied not only physiotherapy during his playing days, but also obtained a degree in human movement. Footballers are not generally known for their academic prowess, just a couple of decent A-Levels can earn you the nickname *'Professor'*, so goodness knows what they call you if you have two university degrees!

Having suffered a ruptured anterior cruciate ligament playing for Blackpool, from which he had failed to recover, he had not expected to play again. Indeed, rumours say that during the scan for this damage, Holden discovered that he had ruptured his posterior cruciate ligament in the same knee ten years previously but had continued to play through the pain for a decade unaware of the seriousness of the injury. However news that one of the best creative footballers in the British Isles is living on your doorstep, doesn't happen every day. The demand for Holden to turn out for any number of local teams was unprecedented. Deciding on Peel FC, also taking on a coaching role at the club and carrying on with his newly found professional endeavours at the same time, Holden inadvertantly qualified himself to play for the Manx national side.

Having seen Holden play in his pomp, turning out for my hometown club, it was strange but wonderful to watch him skinning and tricking professional players time and again - and from only a few feet away. It was like a step back in time and something few of us will ever experience. First time we heard his name on the teamsheet, we turned to each other and said: *"Rick Holden?!...Not THE*

Rick Holden?" but indeed it was. (I guess it's the same experience 30 something women will get in 10 years time when Harry Styles from One Direction is singing in the local pub band.)

A pub band is not actually a bad analogy for the Manx football team. You are as likely to see players from their ranks smoking a pre-match fag, enjoying a pint after the game or walking their dog around the pitch as you are to see them do a proper on-field warm up. But Holden transcended that. It is rare that such a bad team has such genuine and obvious class within it, the red haired maestro pulling the strings and conducting affairs (to mix my orchestral metaphors).

At last there was a genuine chance they could win a game. An outside chance, yes, but a chance all the same. If they came up against leaden-legged opposition, fresh from a 10 mile jog around the coast, then maybe, just maybe they could cause an upset.

And verily it came to pass. Step forward Burnley FC in the year 2000 - Burnley 0 Isle of Man 1. The greatest ever single result achieved in the history of Manx football.

I'm not saying Burnley were going all out for victory, but still they wouldn't be the only team that had gone off half-cock to embarrassing effect.

For example, can you name me the only top flight football team who have played in the Isle of Man Steampacket Festival? (It will take you some time to get even close to coming up with the answer.)

I believe the answer is in fact Watford Football Club, ahead of the 1999/2000 season. I know this for two reasons: 1) I was there 2) Watford is my football team.

Watford had been promoted to the Premier League a couple of months previously after a 2-0 Play Off victory at Wembley over Bolton. Many fans came into this tournament with high hopes. I didn't, due to the fact: 1) I had seen this tournament played before 2) I had seen Watford play before.

I believe we lost both our group games in the Steampacket Festival (one on penalties) and ended up in the wooden spoon play off. I can't remember what happened at this point, but I imagine it ended with us beating the Manx in the play off for last place.

I wasn't overly concerned. After all I would have seen the tournament anyway with or without Watford, so I considered it a bonus to see some of my favourite players. I also got to see my favourite two teams, who both play in yellow tops, red shorts and yellow socks (this is the Manx national kit, as well as Watford's. I actually bought a Manx shirt from Intersport on Strand Street in Douglas one year. They didn't do replica shirts, this was actually one of the tops they had made for the team. I imagine Intersport [who were the team's shirt sponsor at the time] made 25 tops, 22 of which went to the squad and the other three went on general sale due to the national side not wanting them. There is also a bald Millwall fan with tattoos who has one of these shirts - though I guess that is neither helpful or useful info, given that this description covers most Millwall fans).

I also had the distinct advantage over many of my fellow Hornet fans in that, in between games, I had seen many of the younger players scoffing burgers in Griddles and swapping phone numbers with local young ladies of the female persuasion. It was therefore not a surprise to me when winning a tin-pot pre-season tournament wasn't their highest priority out on the pitch.

We have brought up our own daughter properly. Before the age of two she was able to cheer Watford and kiss the club badge; she knew to loudly boo when anyone mentioned our local rivals, Luton Town (irrelevant to whether they were in an airport or on a ferry); and finally never accept propositions from professional footballers, particularly if you are in a cheap burger bar at the time.

The Manx team and wider public would generally admire such lack of commitment to something which is inevitably going to go the way of the pear. For example, one of the most famous Manx national phrases is *"Traa-dy-Liooar"*, this loosely translates to mean *"Time Enough"*. The idea is that there is a time for everything - there is no point rushing around, take your time, all will be well.

In modern parlance though, *"Traa-dy-Liooar"* often more likely means: *"I can't be bothered doing that at the moment"*. As in the following context:

"Juan, can you fix that broken boiler for me?"
"Traa-dy-Liooar, Orry. Traa-dy-Liooar."

I should know more Manx than I do, but my knowledge stretches to the above phrase and also how to say *'toilet'**. (*If you need to know this phrase, it's *'thie veg'* - which sounds like it will be much more fragrant and edible than it actually is.)

For anyone that has attempted to learn a Celtic language - and goodness knows why you would put yourself through that in this day and age - you will always be struck that whilst there are several words for *'wood'* or *'stream'* you will still find yourself having to say *'mobile phone'* and *'helicopter'* due to the lack of ancient Celtic phrases covering such devices.

Incidentally, you would be better off not using a mobile phone on the island. Due to it not being a part of the UK, phone providers will revel in charging you international phone rates for any calls you make. Don't ask how it can be free to make a call from Belfast to London, yet if you are sat in between the two in Douglas it will cost several pounds. There will be some logic, but I'm not seeing it.

The Isle of Man Steampacket Football Festival ceased to be in the last few years. It is an ex-Tournament. Sad, but inevitable due to the growing professionalism in the game and the dwindling number of tourists willing to make the trip.

But somewhere in my heart there will be a place for those brave, hardy and, OK, not especially talented footballers from the Manx national football team. They tried, even if they rarely succeeded.

Let us all commemorate this moment by joining together in singing the national anthem....No, not *God Save The Queen*, not *your* anthem, but the anthem of this plucky island nation: *Land Of Our Birth.*

A one two three....

> *O land of our birth,*
> *O gem of God's earth,*
> *O Island so strong and so fair;*
> *Built firm as Barrule,*
> *Thy Throne of Home Rule*
> *Makes us free as thy sweet mountain air.*

When Orry, the Dane,
In Mannin did reign,
'Twas said he had come from above;
For wisdom from Heav'n
To him had been giv'n
To rule us with justice and love.

Our fathers have told
How Saints came of old,
Proclaiming the Gospel of Peace;
That sinful desires,
Like false Baal fires,
Must die ere our troubles can cease.

Ye sons of the soil,
In hardship and toil,
That plough both the land and the sea,
Take heart while you can,
And think of the Man
Who toiled by the Lake Galilee.

When fierce tempests smote
That frail little boat,
They ceased at His gentle command;

Despite all our fear,
The Saviour is near
To safeguard our dear Fatherland.

Let storm-winds rejoice,
And lift up their voice,
No danger our homes can befall;
Our green hills and rocks
Encircle our flocks,
And keep out the sea like a wall.

Our Island, thus blest, No foe can molest;
Our grain and our fish shall increase;
From battle and sword Protecteth the Lord,
And crowneth our nation with peace.

Then let us rejoice
With heart, soul and voice,
And in The Lord's promise confide;
That each single hour
We trust in His power,
No evil our souls can betide.

To be honest, I thought you'd have picked up

the tune by the eighth verse. Were you not really trying?...That's very Manx, well done!

Now let's go to Griddles.

10. The TT

It would be wrong to write a book about the Isle of Man and not mention the TT races.

The TT is without doubt the embodiment of both sporting greatness and what it means to be Manx. The most famous thing about the Isle of Man is the TT, you can't come here and not embrace the TT. The TT is everything.

I have never seen the TT.

The Isle of Man Tourist Trophy, to give it its full title, is a series of motorbike races held every year on the Isle of Man on its prestigious Mountain Course.

The first TT race was held on Tuesday 28 May 1907, was held on the St John's Short Course, near Tynwald, rather than on the current course. The Mountain Course was first introduced in 1911 but took on it's more recognised form in the 1930s - this is the oldest motor-cycle racing circuit still in use anywhere in the world.

The main reason that I have never seen the TT is that it is held over a two week period between the end of May and the beginning of June - when any self-respecting child will still be in school and therefore unable to travel and enjoy this sporting occasion. (That is unless you are a child who lives in the Isle of Man - if that is the case they give you two weeks off to go and watch some men screaming around on motorbikes as part of your education.)

For two weeks a year, the Isle of Man is transformed. It's not just the large amount of tourists and competitors who flood in, but the sheer logistics of such a massive event on such a small island. If I told you that the Isle of Man is around 30 miles in length and that one lap of the Mountain Course is 37 and three quarter miles of track, you instantly get an idea of the implications.

The TT races are held on public roads, as are the practice sessions, so it is little surprise that during the two week festival the schools, businesses (at least those which are not dependent on the tourist trade) and normal life shuts down. It is hard to get anywhere or do anything - and it is even worse when the races are on!

It's not as bad as it used to be though. In recent years the Manx Government has created a number of relief roads to allow islanders who are stubbornly disinterested in TT racing to get from one town to another, if they so wish. Most locals fully embrace the occasion though. Why not? Buy a leather jacket, jump on a two-wheeler and put some Castrol GTX in your hair. Live a little.

My mum's house was a short walk from the TT course, so there was no escape from the smell and noise of the bikes - and she absolutely loved it. Cronk Gennal was around 100 yards from Quarter Bridge - the big sweeping right hand turn that takes you up towards the dangerous bends at Kirk Michael. The house was actually adjacent to the unnamed section of road which commentators have recently decided to call *"Ago's Leap"* (after former Italian World Champion rider Giacomo Agostini). Whilst I have nothing against Agostini, no-one I have ever met calls this section *"Ago's Leap"*.

This historic course has over 200 bends, most (but not all) of which are named. These bends are easily identified by big orangy-red boards which are dotted around the course, stating the name of the corner and a helpful picture of the geography. I'm not sure how useful this is when you are racing around at speeds of up to 200 miles an hour, but it's great when you are a kid trying to spot them for holiday time entertainment.

Yes, as a child, I would make my Mum drive around the TT course numerous times so I could spot all the famous twists and turns. Not only that we would try to spot every single milestone on the course - quite a feat considering many of this small markers had disappeared or been removed. I never did find a number 3 milestone, and I have the emotional scars to prove it!

I can tell you that none of these boards bore the name *"Ago's Leap"*. It is not a thing.

I am still coming to grips that in 2003 the 32nd milestone corner was renamed *'Dukes'* (after the 1950s world motor-cycle champion Geoff Duke) and the 26th milestone renamed Joey's (after the former Formula 1 TT motor-cycle champion Joey Dunlop) - but at least this was a conscious decision to formally recognise greatness and unrivalled sporting achievement on the island, rather than something a commentator dreamt up one rainy afternoon when he had nothing better to do.

It's a slippery slope to just start randomly naming stuff because you can. For example, I could go around telling everyone that the end of my road is called *"Kerron's Corner"*. It may not be true, but if I keep saying it then my neighbours may start doing the same just in order for a quiet life and to keep me happy - however it does not mean that the end of my road actually is called *"Kerron's Corner"*. This would be a formal decision for my local Council to take.

Obviously, if my local Council want to formally rename the bottom of my road *"Kerron's Corner"* in recognition of all my great works for the community, for my wonderful entertaining writing and for my general good looks and charm, then that is absolutely fine. That would be completely different - and totally understandable.

Of course, by the time this book goes to print (if it ever does go to print), it might be that the Manx Government have formally adopted *"Ago's Leap"* as part of the TT course and erected a giant orangy-red sign. It's not totally out of the question. Earlier this year, the Isle of Man Government took the unusual step of renaming corners after current competitors, with 19 times winner John McGuiness (the most successful racer still competing) and Dave Molyneux (the most successful Manxman) the men honoured. Whilst I think this is wrong-headed and setting a bizarre precedent, they didn't ask me what I thought ahead of making the announcement.

The Isle of Man TT remains the highlight of the motorcycle racing season for racers and fans alike. But it is also one of the most dangerous sporting fixtures anywhere on the planet.

To date there have been over 242 deaths in the TT races since its inception. The roads are fast and the corners harsh and uncompromising. Although hundreds of sandbags adorn each corner of the course, if you get it wrong at high speed on everyday roads, you have as much chance of ending up headfirst in a stone wall, a telegraph pole or over a cliff edge, as you have coming to a safe standstill.

Each year there are calls from the tabloid media, the general do-gooders of society and people like Barry Sheene, calling for the TT to be scrapped due to safety fears - however the reason the races continue, more than any other, is that it is the racers themselves who want to come over year after year to test their skills and nerves against the toughest circuit going.

Would I want to race on the TT course? No. Would I want to ride a motorbike? No. But this shouldn't mean that I should stop other people doing so, especially if this is what they have spent their whole professional careers training to do. There are many things I wouldn't want to do with my life, but each to their own.

Those official fatality figures only include riders killed in races or practices for the TT. They do not include things like marshals and members of the public - let alone members of the public who take part in the annual *"Mad Sunday"* event during TT.

On *"Mad Sunday"*, traditionally the last Sunday before the TT races start in earnest, any member of the public can ride the course and attempt to recreate the exploits of their heroes. Usually members focus on the mountain section of the course, which is open one way from Ramsey to Douglas - but frankly, anything goes. If there were one day a year I would not want to leave the house, or at the very least utilise the new fangled relief roads, this would be it.

I've never been tempted to take on the TT course on two wheels. Predominantly this is because: 1) I don't have a deathwish 2) I don't have a motorbike licence.

My cousin Barry (not technically my cousin, but a relative of my Auntie Eva) was an amateur rider - and a pretty good one. Whilst he never took part in the TT, he did take part in the amateur version of the event, the Manx Grand Prix. We went out to watch him qualify one year. Up at the crack of dawn, freezing to death in the Grandstand on the pit straight (it was August, after all), we cheered him on as he did his best to set a qualifying mark over 5 laps of the Mountain Course.

That year, his bike spluttered out of juice at Windy Corner (a corner named after veteran World Champ, Dave Windy...OK, OK...it's high up on the mountain and can get a bit blowy). But it could have been worse. The year before, having qualified for the main race, he reached the bottom of Bray Hill at the start of Lap One and went flying straight over the stone wall at the bottom and into a massive ditch. His bike was a write-off and he ended up in hospital. To be honest, if this is what happens to someone who is at the top of their game and has trained their whole life for this moment - if they can't make it more than 250 yards into the course without nearly killing themselves, I may give it a miss.

Barry never had another stab at the Grand Prix following the rather disappointing conk out at Windy Corner, but it was probably for the best. He moved to Hong Kong to be a mechanic in professional motorcar racing instead. You may not get the glory in the same way, but you also don't get the risks.

The TT has been in our family from a young age. The nearest I ever got to it when my Great Aunt Kitty (actually my Great Aunt, but not actually a cat), brought me a fluffy koala toy from Australia and I named it *"TT"*. My parents could *'bearly'* believe it.

This was probably inspired by a Children's ITV programme I had seen around that time when CBTV did a dramatised feature on the event.

From what I can remember it involved Roger from *'Rod, Jane and Roger'* fame - who had by this time been replaced on Rainbow by the much younger, thinner and better looking Freddie - being chased around the Isle of Man by an evil villain who had been made up to look and sound Japanese.

It was the 1980s, but it was clearly before the times when blacking up or doing a naff accent was seen as vaguely racially offensive - even if you were just hamming it up for kids. I can clearly remember Roger being abandoned by the Japanese baddie at The Tower of Refuge and jibbering: *"No-one can save you now, not even your Anneka Lice!"*

Yes, Anneka Rice from Treasure Hunt was the love interest. There were also appearances from Mike Smith, and Stephen Frost and Mark Arden from the Carling Black Label adverts. It's amazing that this thing never really took off.

But back to the plot. Roger has come over on the ferry with his prized motorbike - Victor the Velocette - in order to win the TT. (Please note, despite being an amateur, he has somehow been entered into the main TT event and not the Grand Prix specifically designed for amateurs to race in.) He stays overnight with his bike in the expensive Empress Hotel on Douglas seafront, annoying the concierge because he gets oil all over the floor. (Quite how he got his bike up around 100 steps to the hotel reception, past the concierge, let alone up to his bedroom, without being noticed, is never fully explained.) He has not brought his wife with him as she is having an operation on her varicose veins - clearly this is the perfect time to leave her in hospital and give getting himself killed on his bike a spin.

Despite his vintage bike contravening most of the rules about what can and can't enter the modern TT - the scrutineers let him in after he tricks the Chief Scrutineer in a rigged coin-toss. Roger calls *'heads'* because *"Manx coins have no 'tails'."* This is, of course, factually incorrect. Manx coins do have tails - it is the cats which don't have tails (although, as we have covered elsewhere in the book, this is not an entirely true statement either).

Miraculously he is somehow winning the race, until he conks out of juice halfway around the course (not on Windy Corner, but at the Ramsey Gooseneck hairpin). He then gets kidnapped and all matter of hilarious high jinks ensue - whilst we will give this particular side plot a miss for now, he is returned to his bike in order to continue the race. He still has no petrol, so instead fills the bike up with real ale. Apparently this is something that old bikes used to be able to run on, at least in modern fiction, if not real life. His super-powered bike, given this new lease of life, propels itself to an unlikely victory.

Roger wakes up sat in his deckchair at home next to his bike and he discovers it has all been a dream (like Dallas or all bad primary school creative writing). However as he sadly closes the garage door behind him we see the winner's garland hanging up. Hooray!...We never find out if his wife's corrective surgery for the varicose veins has been successful.

I think the idea was probably borrowed from, or inspired by, George Formby's 1935 film

'No Limit'. This was an enjoyable romp that cashed in on the popularity of the TT races in the 1930s, detailing the exploits of a chimney sweep from Wigan who dreams of winning the main prize. (It should not be confused with *'No Limits'* the 1980s BBC2 music show starring Jenny Powell.)

The film is most memorable for the scene where George Formby (playing the chimney sweep turned biker, in case you hadn't guessed) loses control of his bike, after his brakes fail, and careers straight through the crowded bar of the Ballacraine Pub and out the other side before ending up in a field. However the greatest laugh is how the person who directed this film clearly had no idea of the geography of the Isle of Man - as George seamlessly dashes from one end of the island to the other in the time it takes most of us to make a cup of coffee. Quite how he gets down from Douglas Head in time to take part in the races, overtake his rivals, and win the trophy is beyond me. But as George often says: *"It turned out nice again!"*

Something which can rarely ever be said at Snaefell...

11. Snaefell

Snaefell is the highest point of the Isle of Man, standing at 2,034 ft above sea level. It is what is technically known in the trade as a *'Mountain'*.

If you've ever seen that film *'The (English) Man Who Went Up a Hill and Came Down a Mountain'*, it is like that except it is *'The Man Who Went Up a Mountain and Came Down A Mountain, Because It's a Mountain'*.

Snaefell gets its name from the old Norse lexicon and apparently when loosely translated, the phrase means *'Snow Mountain'*.

I actually think it's a mistranslation and that it was probably called *'Fog Mountain'* back in the day, but I have absolutely no evidence for this.

However I do know that *'fog'* is a Danish corruption of the old Norse word *'fok'* meaning *'spray'*, *'shower'*, *'snowdrift'* - all of which could aptly describe the usual experience of an afternoon up Snaefell.

I am guessing the Manx authorities persuaded their Viking overlords to avoid going with *'Fok-fell'* because it sounds too much like what someone might utter if they tripped over on their way up and slid down the steep mountainside. I can here it echoing around the island now: *"Aargh...Fok...Fell..."*

It is said that on a clear day six kingdoms can be seen from the top: The Kingdom of Mann (the Isle of Man), The Kingdom of England, The Kingdom of Ireland (clearly this predates the North-South split), The Kingdom of Scotland, The Kingdom of Wales and The Kingdom of Heaven.

You may think that *'The Kingdom of Heaven'* is a bit of a cheat (especially as there is no way you can see Vicarage Road Stadium from this summit), but in this ancient adage *'heaven'* is referring to the skies overhead rather than any deeper theological context.

I suppose you could push the boat out and say that you can see a seventh kingdom, The Kingdom of Manannan (the kingdom of the seas surrounding this island nation), but why you would want to push your boat out into this kingdom if you know Manannan is there under the surface ready to pop out at a moment's notice? That mythical sea god throws islands, don't you know. That must be a clear health and safety concern.

In reality there is normally only one kingdom you can see from the summit of Snaefell - The Kingdom of Fog.

However, even if visibility is poor, there is a helpful sign at the summit telling you what should be out there beyond the greyness. I guess they do this much in the same spirit that Jim Bowen used to tell two sheet-metal workers from Keighley, at the end of Bullseye: *"Let's look at what you could have won."* It is an unreachable fantasy, an unattainable dream which sits behind a wall of cheap MDF or mist (depending on the metaphor), it screams *"Ha, ha, pal...you will never own a speedboat or see the Mountains of Mourne!"* In short, it is neither helpful or desirable in the circumstances. It is not the sort of behaviour that polite society should endorse or encourage. It is the sort of thoughtless faux pas that could end with someone getting a smack in the mouth, or at the very least a plinth being daubed in sweary graffiti.

For what it's worth, Snaefell is the following distance from its neighbouring countries:

31 miles from the Mull of Galloway (Scotland)
51 miles from Scafell (England)
66 miles from the Mountains of Mourne (Northern Ireland)
and 97 miles from Dublin.

Great, smashing, super, brill. Give them a round of applause.

You will note that the above list does not include reference to the nearest spot in Wales, but a quick check of my Atlas* tells me that it is 59 miles to Amlwch in Anglesey.

(*OK, I Googled it, but that doesn't sound nearly as impressive.)

If you are travelling between April and October, during the height of Summer Season, than you can take an electrical tram to the top of Snaefell. This is probably the wisest and least breezy choice.

The Snaefell Mountain Railway is a branch of the Manx Electric Railway and was established in 1895. It looks like the other sections of MER aside from two key differences: 1) Due to the steep inclines, a third rail is used in the centre of the tracks to add stability and greater traction 2) Due to the consistently poor weather and extreme conditions, on each tram a pair of closed carriages is used - there is absolutely no demand for open-sided carriages, not even from foolhardy tourists.

The Snaefell Mountain Railway is 5 miles in length and runs from Laxey station up to the summit station, via the Bungalow request stop. The trip takes around 30 minutes in either direction.

For those wanting to hike up Snaefell there is a rough path to the peak which runs directly up the side of the mountain from the Bungalow. It's a challenging walk and not suitable for families - partly due to the difficulty of the trail and partly due to the bad language that any children present may be unwittingly subjected to. On a dry day, this climb should take around 45 minutes. On a wet day, just don't bother.

The Bungalow is one of the highest points on the TT course. It seems incredible that bikes doing top speed over this section of the course would have to thunder over a section of tramlines, but that is indeed the case. You don't get that anywhere else in the world, do you. Perhaps that should move the British

Formula One Grand Prix from Silverstone to Blackpool sea front? That would make it a more interesting race.

The name derives from the now defunct and demolished Bungalow Hotel. The Swiss Chalet design, modular-kit wood-built structure with corrugated roof, stood on the site from 1900 to 1958. Now all that is left, aside from the name, is a small tram shelter.

During race days, the Snaefell Mountain Railway service is broken into two parts with passengers having to disembark and cross a footbridge over the racecourse to pick up a connecting service to the top. Not even the TT organisers would make racers dodge trams half way round the circuit, though I do think it would make a nice addition to the TT Crazy Golf Course.

A hundred yards or so up the hill are another set of buildings. These used to belong to the Ministry of Defence, but for many years following the war, these were the home of

Murray's Motorcycle Museum.

I loved the Murray's Motorcycle Museum. Not only were there every sort of motorbike you could imagine from the early 1800s to the present, there were also all manner of other distractions such as Victorian style penny arcade machines. This may not sound that unusual but these old machines were something to behold, real feats of engineering, and to get them to work you had to use an old Victorian penny - rather than any form of new currency.

Sadly, a sign on the building now indicates that this may not have been the wisest marketing tool:

"CLOSED PERMANENTLY! Due to lack of demand, as of Oct 2005 this museum has closed."

Do they sound bitter much?

If only they had converted those machines to

take a crisp new £5 note rather than old Victorian penny, and they might have been on to a winner.

Stepping inside that building was like stepping back in time. For example, the walls were covered in old 19th and 20th Century advertising posters. You don't get that it most other tourist shops here, though you can still buy things like traditional Manx Ices (though not the recipe outlawed by European legislation in the 1980s) and suck on a Manx Knob (the traditional humbug sweet, popular throughout the island - rather than anything more provocative, I'm afraid).

Talking of knobs, I once saw the cast of Top Gear here - outside the old motorcycle museum - recording features for their hilariously sexist and borderline xenophobic Sunday night show. I say *'cast'* rather than *'presenters'* because it is the most heavily scripted show currently on the BBC. It makes Eastenders look like a bunch of Thespians doing improvisations through the medium of scowl.

There are two reasons I can think for Top Gear wanting to come to the Isle of Man: 1) Jeremy Clarkson lives here. At least he does when he isn't spending his time chin-wagging with his equally charming neighbour David Cameron in Chipping Norton. Clarkson married a Manx woman 20 years ago. I am just eternally grateful that it wasn't my Mum. They live in a lighthouse at Langness, near Castletown - he probably has a car in Oxfordshire with a bumper sticker that says *"My other home is a lighthouse!"*. Apparently some locals didn't immediately warm to him due to a dispute over closing and rerouting public footpaths outside his property. He claimed having a public footpath so close to his lighthouse breached his human rights - ignoring that the footpath had probably been in place before his property existed and certainly before he moved into it - the judge disagreed and in 2012 the public right of way was reinstated. 2) There is no upper speed limit for motor vehicles on certain parts of the island.

It is one of the well-trodden myths that there are no speed limits whatsoever in the Isle of Man. Indeed, the island was one of the first places in the British Isles to adopt 20 mph speed limit zones in residential areas around schools. However it is true that there are no speed limits on the mountain roads between Ramsey and Douglas - many of which are part of the TT course. Quite why you would want to do between 100 mph and 200 mph on twisty section of road, with poor visibility, is beyond me. Anyone hitting such speeds has as much chance of ending up in the sea as they have setting a new land-speed record.

That day at the Bungalow, the Stig was getting in something that looked like a cross between a go kart and a racing car. I could have told them how dangerous berking about at high speeds is, but I thought *"Nah, let them find out for themselves"* as I was in a tram.

I promised earlier in the book to tell you about Accident Black Spots, so here you go. Throughout the 1970s and 1980s (indeed, maybe even before this, but I wasn't born so it's difficult for me to confirm either way) the Manx Government would mark spots where there had been a large number of fatal accidents to encourage motorists to cut their speeds and pay more attention to the roads.

They decided the best way to do this was to erect a series of brightly coloured signs at the sites in question. The traditional Manx Accident Black Spot signs were a red triangle with a yellow background and a black circle in the middle, accompanied by black text saying *"ACCIDENT BLACK SPOT"*.

Sadly these often had a counterproductive effect as so many people would be distracted by the brightly coloured signs, and as a result would go careering off the road. As a child I would spend many hours searching for them. The signs, not the crashed motorists. Ironically, the worst accident blackspot, *"The*

Blackboards" (between Santon and Castletown), did not have an Accident Blackboard Sign - they simply had a white and black board telling you to slow down. That's how it got its name - though I doubt that *"The Red and Yellow Triangle with a Black Spot Sign"* would have made the junction much safer.

So kids, mind how you go, and don't do drugs.

Of course, the signs became redundant with the advent of speed cameras. Not only could you get people to slow down, you could make a nice profit out of them too.

If you do manage to reach the top of Snaefell without dying, there is a Summit Hotel and cafe. I recommend a hot bowl of soup and a pint of something refreshing. There isn't much beyond that - indeed, it's all downhill from there.

About the Author –

Kerron Cross was born on 21st August 1977 in High Wycombe, but was raised just outside Watford, to a Manx Mum and a Lancastrian Dad. A published writer in many fields and genres – his first book *"Drama, Verse, Sketches 2"* was published in 2001, published by CPAS Publishing and co-authored with Steve Tilley. As a professional speechwriter, he has written articles for most of the UK national newspapers (both tabloid and broadsheet), as well as written for and appeared on TV, radio and online platforms. He worked for 10 years in the Houses of Parliament for two very nice MPs, spent some time working in Manchester for a Government Minister and then spent 4 years working for an Archbishop! He has also stood for Parliament in the 2005 General Election in the socialist stronghold of South West Hertfordshire and has 8 years' experience as a councillor on a local authority. He supports Watford FC (for his sins), Wigan RL and Lancashire CC. He is married to a Glaswegian and has a daughter called Blythe.

CPSIA information can be obtained
at www.ICGtesting.com
Printed in the USA
LVOW10s1042010717

540041LV00011B/690/P